JESUS CHRIST AND THE TEMPLE

GEORGES BARROIS

JESUS CHRIST
AND
THE TEMPLE

ST. VLADIMIR'S SEMINARY PRESS
CRESTWOOD, NEW YORK 10707
1980

Library of Congress Cataloging in Publication Data

Barrois, Georges Augustin, 1898-
  Jesus Christ and the temple.

  Includes bibliographical references.
  1. Temple of God. I. Title.
BS680.T4B37   262   80-19700
ISBN 0-913836-73-7

PRINTED IN THE UNITED STATES OF AMERICA

BY

ATHENS PRINTING COMPANY
461 Eighth Avenue
New York, NY 10001

Contents

Foreword

This little book, the third I am writing for the St. Vladimir's Seminary Press, is not a work of erudition. I have no intention of stating here everything we know, directly or indirectly, concerning the arrangement and liturgy of the temple of Jerusalem, nor to write a new chapter of Orthodox theology. The problem before us is rather: What did the temple, its solemn assemblies, its festive processions, represent for the common people in the time of Jesus? What did the temple mean to the twelve-year-old boy who ascended with his parents to the holy city "after the custom of the feast" (Luke 2:42)? As a grown-up man, he left his carpenter-shop of Nazareth to spread his Gospel throughout the land. In Jerusalem, shortly before his death, he wondered with his followers at the size and the perfection of the stone masonry of the temple, as they sat in the sparse shade of a tree on the slope of the Mount of Olives, facing the monumental constructions of the Herodian architects.

The temple had been a beacon of light shining through centuries of darkness, and Israel was the guardian of the flame until he would appear, who was to appear. Some four decades after the Cross and the Resurrection, the temple was destroyed. It would not be rebuilt. A new era, of cosmic proportion, was being ushered in. The old was over. "The form of this world passes away," wrote St. Paul (1 Cor 7:31). The Jews would continue to lament over the ruins of the temple, expecting the advent of the Messiah — or of a de-personalized Messiah — in an indefinite future. For us the long vigil has ended. Jesus Christ, the Jerusalem pilgrim, having satisfied in himself all the requirements of the Law, initiated the new age announced by the prophets; it dawned over the empty sepulchre where life was reborn. We stand "between the times", heading toward the final triumph, whose hour has been decided in the secret counsel of the Trinity. This is what we should bear constantly in mind.

In the pages that follow, biblical quotations are given from the King James Version (KJ), the Revised Standard (RSV), or in my own rendering of the Hebrew or Greek. The numbering of chapters and verses is that of the English Bibles. I did not feel obligated to cling to one single text, but I must apologize for whatever inconsistencies due to oversight or neglect on my part. I wish at this point to remind eventual readers of the fact that the Apocrypha and Deuterocanonical Books are now available in handy editions, either *The Holy Bible: An Ecumenical Edition* or *The Oxford Annotated Bible with the Apocrypha.*

I shall use the forms of the divine name agreed upon by the majority of biblical scholars: Yahweh, Elohim, Adonaï; in literal quotations, I generally follow the usage of the English versions: "the Lord", "the Lord God". I shall retain the conventional spelling of the King James or the Revised Standard Version for those names of persons or places which have passed into current English vocabulary.

Some confusion in toponymy may result from the contemporary political and ethnological problems involving the modern Israeli state and the status of the Palestinians. I shall use "Palestine" as a convenient designation for the territories limited to the east by the Jordan river, the Dead Sea, and the 'Arabah; to the north, by Mount Hermon; and to the south by the Sinai peninsula. It corresponds roughly to the biblical stereotype "from Dan to Beersheba" or the less precise "from the entrance of Hamath to the brook of Egypt." We should keep in mind that the name Israel designates primarily the *religious* community instituted by Moses and, as a later *political* quantity, the schismatic kingdom of the north, from Jeroboam to the fall of Samaria in 722 B.C.

The maps found at the end of the *Jerusalem Bible* or the *Ecumenical Bible*, and the maps, plans and illustrations in the various atlases of the Holy Land, or in biblical dictionaries such as the *Interpreter's Dictionary the Bible*, will be helpful for an understanding of the chapters relative to the holy places of the Hebrews, the temples, and the episodes of Jesus' life.

I owe to the friendship of my colleagues of the Ecole Biblique de Jérusalem and the courtesy of the Editions J. Gabalda and Co., Paris, the permission to use the drawings of the late Fr. Vincent and of Fr. Steve, in connection with Ch. 3, "The Temples of Jerusalem".

I wish to make it clear that I am not writing for professional theologians, exegetes, or archeologists. Let specialists follow each one his own line. Personally, I am a staunch believer in the cross-fertilization of various intellectual approaches, as long as the integrity of proper methods is safeguarded. I have been working primarily but not exclusively for my Orthodox brothers and sisters in our seminaries, in colleges and universities, for all who prepare themselves for the service of the Church or who are engaged in teaching our young people. To them I dedicate this little book. My thanks go to all who have encouraged me, manifested their interest, and helped me in the preparation, typing and polishing of the manuscript.

CHAPTER ONE

Early Hebrew Sanctuaries

Our principal source is the Bible of the Old and New Testament. Only through it do we gain some understanding of the religion of the temple, sacred to all the sons of Abraham; Jesus was a son of Abraham according to his human birth, and the temple became the scene of the decisive moments of his life. If we consider that the first appearance of Abraham and his clan has been dated with great probability to the first half of the second millenium, toward 1700 B.C.— so late in history! — a question comes immediately to mind: "And what happened before?" The scribes of the temple who collected the traditions of Moses toward the end of the Israelite monarchy and completed their work during the Exile had no sources of information enabling them to answer this question. They were up to the problem of how to bridge the gap between the appearance of man on earth and the first lineaments of history, howsoever vague.[1] They drew largely on the literary records of their Middle East neighbors, a mixture of fact and fiction.

The first part of Genesis, the "Book of Origins", is rich in episodes reflecting these common traditions: organization of the cosmos from the primitive chaos, the Flood, the Tower of Babel, the confusion of tongues, the distinction of races,

---

[1] A case in point is the extraordinary longevity of the patriarchs. Adam is said to have lived 930 years; Seth, 912; Enoch, 905; Lamech, the bigamous, 777. After the flood, Noah, head of a new race of men, 950 years; Terah, Abraham's father, 205; Abraham himself, 175 years. Reading upwards, it is obvious that the absolute beginning will never be reached. The figures in the Hebrew text differ from those given in the Septuagint and the Samaritan Pentateuch, suggesting speculations, probably of a symbolical nature, which escape us. See detailed tables and explanations in the *Interpreter's Bible*, vol. I, pp. 142-144.

and similar features, thoroughly "demythologized" by the Hebrew scribes, who used them as a vehicle for their unique faith, namely their belief in one God the Creator and in His plan for mankind: the first couple, its estrangement from God through sin, the promise of a Savior who would heal the old wound and restore the broken relationship between men and their Maker. The authors of Genesis expressed their own understanding of the progress of civilization and the development of monotheism in the pre-patriarchal age, not without anachronisms, artificial etymologies of person- or place-names, and fragments of popular legends.[2]

We are tempted to ask here another question: Are we committed to holding the world-view of the Semites and specifically of the Hebrews? Other people had a different conception of the evolution of the world and of the growth of human civilization; why rather the Semitic version, as interpreted by the scribes of Israel? The only answer we can give is that Judaism and Christianity are historical religions. Not that our faith is measured by history, but because God spoke through historical events, and entered history in the person of Jesus Christ. "In the beginning was the Word. . . . and the Word was made flesh." We are bound, willy-nilly, to watch the panorama of history from the vantage point of biblical culture, if we are to perceive the values of the Judeo-Christian revelation unto life, whereas the scientist and the historian aim at a more extensive analysis, but of itself neutral and non-committal, of cosmic and human phenomena.

This commands our approach: we must proceed with a careful scrutiny of the Semitic past while knowing at the same time that a purely rational conclusion is excluded, for our goal is not to build a system, but to shape our faith. A wild chase through the ancient cultures of the Near- and Middle East, a hunt for fragments or parallels from other civilizations may be impressive and at times useful, but can in no way be a substitute for the revelational experience conveyed by the biblical authors.

[2] Seeking a correspondance between the *saga* of primitive mankind and the positive findings of anthropology and prehistory is methodologically unsound; so-called "concordism" is bad science and bad theology.

As for the relation of the Old Testament to the New Testament revelation, two extreme positions must be avoided: on the one hand, to imagine a radical break between the Gospel and the Bible of the Hebrews as if God had suddenly changed his mind, and conclude that we may as well dispense with the study of the latter — a mild form of heresy, suiting our prejudice or . . . our laziness. On the other hand, while the face of the "Christ of faith" appears as through transparence in the Old Testament, the relation of the new dispensation of grace to the ancient economy of salvation is not to be understood as a continuous flowing of the "old" into the "new". There is a fundamental difference between the regimen of the Law and the life of grace, Israel and the Church; one passes from the one to the other as the fathers of old passed from the centuries before the Law to the legal institutions of the Mosaic age through a series of transformations which can be compared with biological transmutations within the same species, or with the transpositions of the same musical theme. We have to cope with entirely new situations created by the uniqueness of the Incarnation.

As much as we dislike lifeless theorizing, we believe that the above considerations may prove, if not necessary, at least useful to avoid misconceptions, as we are to review the religion of the patriarchs and their places of worship, in order to outline the pre-history of Moses' tabernacle and Solomon's temple.

THE HEBREW PATRIARCHS. The "descent" of the Hebrews into Canaan is part of a migration of Aramaean peoples from Mesopotamia, who settled on the crescent-shaped band of cultivable lands on border of the Syrian steppe and in the districts of what is now Syria, whereas the Phenicians held the Mediterranean seaboard. Genesis 11:31 relates how Terah, Abraham's father, left the fields of Ur of the Chaldees in southern Mesopotamia and followed in the path of the migrating Aramaeans. Abraham, pressing further ahead, reached the land of Canaan where, together with his kinsmen, he continued living as a nomadic shepherd, driving his flocks of sheep on the semi-desertic pastures east and south of what would later be called Samaria and Judaea.

The route of the Aramaean migration had been staked at each stage by sanctuaries dedicated to the moon-god and his retinue of deities worshipped throughout the Semitic lands. But Genesis 12:1 states expressly that Abraham was led by a higher light. His age was an age of transition: transition from polytheism to monotheism, no matter under which name the one God of the Hebrews would henceforth be known; transition from the Aramaean ethnic group to a new people having a distinct individuality, which would later be called Israel and infiltrate, overrun and finally absorb the indigenous populations of Canaan; linguistic transition, from Aramaic to Hebrew.

This manifold metamorphosis, religious, ethnic, and linguistic, was to take several generations. We should not find it strange that the revealed monotheism of the patriarchs continued expressing itself in forms and rituals common among the Semites. It simply could not have been otherwise; similarities of ritual do not necessarily imply identical beliefs.

The Book of Genesis enumerates the major stations of the Hebrews in Canaan, distributed along the main north-south road of central Palestine. The western slopes drain toward the Mediterranean seaboard; the steeper eastern slopes, arid and semi-desertic, toward the depression of the Jordan and of the Dead Sea, providing meager pastures for the Hebrew shepherds. In a marked contrast, the western slopes offered to the Canaanite villagers relatively fertile hillsides and valleys fit for terrace cultivations: olive-groves, vineyards, cereals and, wherever the water supply, always rare, permitted it, orchards and vegetable gardens. While the nomadic shepherds wandered about in quest of grazing areas according to the rhythm of the seasons, their chieftains came into contact with the Canaanites in the market centers along the trunk road, such as Shechem, Bethel, Hebron, and Beer-sheba (Be'êr-Sheba') in the Negeb, where they exchanged the products of their herds against grain supplies and other commodities.

SHECHEM. The first encampment of the Hebrews on this side of the Jordan had been under the walls of Shechem, in the pass between Mount Gerizim and Mount Ebal,[3] a prime location. Branching out from the main artery, a side road rounding Mount Ebal to the south-east descends along the perennial stream of the Wâdi Fâr'a to the fords of the Jordan. or from Transjordan and the Gôlân. A short notice of the Book of Genesis (12:6-7) records Abraham's journey to Canaan "unto Shechem, unto the Oak of Môreh." Môreh, a proper noun, may mean, according to a far-from-certain etymology, "the teacher", "the soothsayer"; the Greek version has a common adjective instead: "unto the lofty oak tree".[4] We might intepret: "the oak of the [divine] Revealer". At any rate the text refers to a tree venerated by the local people for its supernatural virtue. Such "sacred" trees were regular features of Canaanite holy places. Now Yahweh manifested his presence to Abraham at the Oak of Môreh, and there Abraham built an altar to the God who had appeared to him. This is the first reported case of appropriation of a Canaanite sanctuary by the Hebrews.

The next mention that is made of Shechem is found in the story of Jacob (Gen 33:18-20). The context is as follows: Jacob, after his definitive separation from his Aramaean in-laws and his much apprehended meeting with Esau, the wild man of Edom, "came to the town of Shechem and camped before the town". We are told that the town had been named for a certain Shechem, of the sons of Hamor, "the Ass". Jacob purchased "the piece of land where he had pitched his tent, and erected an altar which he named El-Elohê-Israel"; that is: "'El', the common name of the Deity among the Semites, "God of Israel". According to the theophany recorded in Genesis 32:28, "Israel" is the God-given name of Jacob; in the time of Moses it would designate the people issued from his twelve sons. Thus the old Canaanite holy place had now

[3] Shechem is identified with *Tell el-Balâta*, excavated by German archaeologists, approximately one mile from the center of modern Nablus, left of the high road when travelling toward Jerusalem.

[4] The Latin Vulgate, using another basic text, reads: *usque ad convallem illustrem*, "unto the noble valley". Note the hybrid translation of KJ: "unto the plain of Môreh".

become the legal possession of the Hebrews in the "Land of Promise".

The sanctuary at Shechem figures once more in Genesis 35:2-5, when Jacob left the place, fearing reprisal of the local people after a treacherous assault on the Shechemites by two of his sons. Before departing, he buried under the sacred oak all the foreign gods and the ear-rings which the members of his household had smuggled out the Aramaean country (cf. Gen:31:32-35).[5] The order he gave them to "purify themselves and to change their garments" (35:2) implies a radical break from the heathen past. God's response was the supernatural terror which fell on the Shechemites and made them renounce pursuing the sons of Jacob.

A notice in the Book of Joshua closes the tradition of Shechem as a holy place of the patriarchs (Jos. 24:32): the bones of Joseph, which the Israelites brought up from Egypt, were buried "in the piece of land which Jacob had bought from the sons of Hamor, the father of Shechem. . . . and it became the inheritance of the sons of Joseph." Local traditions have preserved the memory of Joseph's resting place. A cenotaph under the cupola of a small Moslem shrine is venerated as being the tomb of Joseph. Competing with the Shechem tradition which avails itself of the testimony of the Book of Joshua, the rival tradition of Hebron locates the tomb of Joseph in the cave of Machpelah, where the other patriarchs had been laid to rest.

The Fourth Gospel, relating the conversation of Jesus with the Samaritan woman (John 4:7-26), refers to the well dug, according to local tradition, by Jacob himself, "who drank from it, and his sons, and his cattle"; it is not mentioned in the narratives of Genesis. It must have been located at a short distance from the ancient city wall, near "the parcel of land which Jacob gave to his son Joseph" (John 4:5). The deep well of living water which is shown to pilgrims in the crypt of the Greek church has every chance of being authentic.

BETHEL. The next station of the patriarchs in Canaan is

---

[5] The hiding of the domestic idols brought from Aram does not seem to constitute a "sacrifice of foundation" as it has been suggested by some critics.

Bethel, some 29 miles south of Shechem. The ancient site underlies the modern village of Beitîn and could not be excavated wholesale. According to Genesis 12:8-9, Abraham had camped nearby. He had built an altar to Yahweh and called on his name, "having Bethel to the west and Aï (*'Aï*) to the east." [6] This is Abraham's second sanctuary, second altar. Soon he journeyed on, down to the winter pastures of the Negeb. In the spring, he would stop again at his Bethel camp (Gen 13:2). There he parted from his nephew Lot who thus far had travelled with him, from Haran. Quarrels between their shepherds had made this move advisable. Lot would henceforth pasture his flocks in the lower part of the depression of the Jordan, today the basin of the Dead Sea, *Bahr Lût*, "the sea of Lot" in Arabic toponymy (Gen 13:8-13).[7] This is an early instance of the tendency of the Hebrews to form on the soil of Canaan a group of their own, distinct from the Aramaeans. They "Canaanized" their names; thus Abram became Abraham, Saraï became Sarah. Two generations later, the story of the agreement between Jacob and his Aramaean relatives is symptomatic: they built a cairn of fieldstones as a landmark for the delimitation of pasture grounds on the tableland across Jordan. Laban the Aramaean called it in Aramaic *Yegar-sa' adûthâ*, Jacob called it in Hebrew *Gal'êd* (Gilead), the meaning in either case being "the cairn-in-witness" (Gen 31:47-48).

Bethel was to become the sanctuary of Jacob par excellence. Two passages of Genesis are of capital importance for the origin of the sanctuary (Gen 28:10-19 and 35:1-15). Jacob's decision to leave Shechem, where his sons had made themselves undesirable to the Canaanite burghers (Gen

---

[6] 'Aï, in Hebrew, with the article, *hâ-'Aï*, cf. the Greek ʿAγγαï, "the ruin", is identified with *et-Tell*, ca. 2 miles east-southeast of Beitîn, on a secondary road leading down toward Jericho. The site, excavated from 1933 to 1935, had been occupied since 3000 B.C. but was destroyed toward 2000 B.C. and deserted since; thus it was already "the ruin" in the time of the patriarchs. Two groups of ruins between Beitîn and et-Tell may be the remains of a Byzantine monastery, mentioned by St. Jerome, commemorating Jacob's dream, and of a church marking the location of Abraham's altar.

[7] The author of Genesis supposes that the southern part of the Jordan valley, which had been "like a garden of Yahweh", was submerged following the cataclysm which destroyed the sinful cities of Sodom and Gomorrha.

34:30), and to go and pitch his tent near Bethel, was not a step into the unknown, but in a sense a pilgrimage to the place where his grandfather had camped.

Genesis 28:10-19 relates how in his youth Jacob had been sent by his parents to take a wife from among their Aramaean relatives; his absence from the family home might also placate the resentment of his older brother Esau, whom he had repeatedly cheated more than is permissible. Weary from the journey, he stopped one evening on the roadside for an overnight rest. He had a dream: a ladder was set up on the earth and reached to heaven; angels were ascending and descending, and Yahweh stood on top and said: "I am Yahweh God of Abraham thy father and God of Isaac." Jacob, waking up from his sleep, said: "Surely Yahweh is in this place and I did not know! . . . How awesome is this place; it is none else but the house of God and the gate of heaven." Then he took the stone on which he had rested his head, set it up as a pillar, and anointed it with oil. We find in this story an etymology of Bethel, *beth-'el,* οἶκος Θεοῦ, "house of God", and a characteristic feature of Jacob's sanctuaries: the sacred pillar or stela, in Hebrew *matsêbah,* pl. *matsêboth,* στήλη. He would erect such *matsêboth* in Gilead and in Ephrath (Bethleem-Ephrata).

We turn now to Genesis 35:1-15. The entire passage is composed of fragments drawn from a variety of sources. The notice on Bethel begins with a flashback to the episode of Jacob's dream. The etymology of Bethel, formerly Lûz, is confirmed: "He called the place 'El Beth-'el," that is to say: God, or the God of Bethel, namely the Deity which appeared to Jacob and unto which he dedicated an altar, as he had already done at Shechem. God is identified in verse 11 as *'El-Shaddaï*; the name, tentatively interpreted by some exegetes as "God of the mountains" (Akkadian *shâdê*), is omitted in the Greek or interpreted in other passages as Παντοκράτωρ or Ἱκανός, the "Almighty" or the "Self-sufficient", *Deus Omnipotens* (Vulg.), "God Almighty". Verse 14 repeats 28:18 f: erection of a stone pillar, *matsêbah,* on which Jacob pours a libation and which he anoints with oil. The tomb of Deborah, the nurse of Rebekah, Jacob's mother, is mentioned in connection with the sanctuary, "beneath Bethel", under an oak known as the *'allôn bâkûth*, "the oak of weeping". The change of the name of Jacob into Israel, previously related to the episode of "prevailing upon God", was now linked with the foundation of the sanctuary at Bethel.

HEBRON. Travelling south along the Great Road with the patriarchs, we leave on the left the acropolis of the Jebusites — David's future capital — and reach Hebron, some thirty miles distant from Bethel. Hebron is the center around which the entire activity of Abraham in Canaan revolved, just as Bethel became the sanctuary of Jacob-Israel. Abraham, after his separation from Lot, had established his camp "at the oak, or oaks, of Mamrê, and built there an altar unto Yahweh" (Gen 13:18). We notice the same hesitation of the versions as in the sections on Shechem: oak, oaks, terebinth, the Vulgate's *convallis illustris* and "the plain of Mamrê" (KJ). A revelation of Yahweh is at the origin of the sanctuary. The message is clear; it is an "Annunciation". Sarah, Abraham's wife, will conceive in her old age and bear him the long-expected son, Isaac. It is at the same time an advance notice of the cataclysm which wiped out the city of Sodom in spite of Abraham's plea that it be spared, "if only fifty..., forty..., thirty..., twenty..., ten righteous men, were found in it", a condition which was not met. The scenario is simple: Abraham is sitting at the entrance of his tent "in the heat of the day". Three men appear, whom he treats lavishly, as befits a chieftain of his rank. After the meal, he shows them the road to Sodom, the sinful city to which they are sent as executors of God's judgments. Only Lot and Lot's daughters will escape the disaster.

We are puzzled by the fluctuations of the text regarding the personality of the messengers. In Genesis 18:1, Yahweh, ὁ κύριος, appears to Abraham; 18:2, three men present themselves at the entrance of Abraham's tent; 18:3, (Abraham speaking), "My Lord", *'Adônaï*, Κύριε) ; [8] 18:16, the

---

[8] These nouns are not necessarily interpreted as proper nouns. *'Adônaï* could be vocalized *'adôni* "my lord", "sir", as would κύριε, domine. However the form *'Adônaï* is often used as a substitute for the not-to-be-pronounced divine name.

same three men again as in verse 2; 18:17, Yahweh himself,
pronouncing the sentence against the Sodomites; 18:33, "And
Yahweh went his way"; 19:1, "two angels", or "the two
angels"; 19:11-13, "the men" are reported saying: "We will
destroy this place"; 19:14, Lot imputes the cataclysm to
Yahweh himself. This shifting of subjects has been tentatively
regarded as evidence for a plurality of sources fused into a
single story by the final redactor; yet it does not look like a
mosaic. Or would Yahweh be one of the three, as the principal actor of the drama, escorted by two attendants, the two
angels of 19:1? Then the text could speak alternately of one,
or two, or three supernatural beings. This simple arithmetic
might solve the riddle. It seems more likely, however, that
the redactor, presumably a Jewish scholar of priestly caste,
felt embarrassed by the anthropomorphisms of the primitive
tradition: think of Yahweh eating roasted veal in Abraham's
tent! The hesitations of the text would reflect his theological
scruples. The patristic tradition saw in the three who appeared
to Abraham a figure of the Trinity. *Tres vidit, et unum ador-
avit*, "Three he saw, One he adored." The angels of Rublev's
"Old Testament Trinity" sitting at the mystical table are the
most eloquent pictorial translation of the theophany at the
oaks of Mamrê.

We have already noticed the practice of burying notable
members of the tribe in the vicinity of their place of worship;
the tombs of the ancestors and the living members of the clan
are placed under the protection of the divinity, in the shadow
of the sacred tree, close to the altar upon which the sacrifices
are offered to their God and in memory of the dead. Thus the
cave of Machpelah in Hebron, where Sarah and Abraham,
their sons and daughters, were laid to rest, completes the
sanctuary, although it is distant from the oaks of Mamrê, the
so-called *Haram Râmet el-Khalîl*,[9] by two and a half miles.
Like Mamrê, the Machpelah would become a place of pilgrimage; it seems to have been visited by the Jews as early as the
monarchy, and it continued to be frequented in hellenistic

[9] *El-Khalîl*, the "friend of God", is the surname given Abraham by the
Arabs, his descendents through Ishmael.

times, under the Romans, and the Byzantine, Frankish, Moslem and Israeli occupation.

Chapter 23 of Genesis describes Abraham's purchase of the cave of Machpelah from Ephron the Hittite, who owned the land into which it opened. The elaborate account of the transaction strikes a note of realism and compares with legal instruments of sale in the cuneiform documents of the time: "The field with the cave in it, all the trees in the field, and all things here-enclosed, are ceded to Abraham in firm possession, in the eyes of the Benê-Heth," for a sum of "four hundred shekels of silver, current traders' weight". The funeral chambers are located under the mosque occupying the southern extremity of a Herodian monumental enclosure, in Arabic toponymy the *Haram el-Khalîl*, under Moslem jurisdiction.

THE HEGEB. Favored by a milder climate than the Judaean highlands, the Negeb offered to the Patriarchs winter pastures to which they drove their sheep and goats at the approach of the cold season. They shared the wells and grazing grounds with herdsmen of various ethnic origins, whom we cannot identify with certainty. The compiler of the Pentateuch was not as successful at organizing the material relative to the Negeb as he had done for the traditions of Shechem, Bethel, and Hebron. The text gives a general impression of disparateness. What seems basically the same story is repeated two or even three times, with only the names of the actors or minimal circumstances being changed. We have also to disregard frequent anachronisms, such as making the Philistines firmly established in the country when the Hebrew nomads appeared first in the Negeb. It remains that a number of episodes witness to a Hebrew center of worship at the wells of Beersheba.

Beersheba is first mentioned in connection with an agreement between Abraham and Abimelech, a chieftain of the region (Gen 21:25-33). There had been some quarrel among their herdsmen about a well claimed by Abraham. The point of the entire story is to explain the etymology of the name of Beersheba. It is interpreted in verses 28-30 as the "well of the Seven", *be'êr shéba'*, in reference to seven ewes brought by Abraham in witness that he had dug the well. We may suppose that these seven ewes were in fact destined to strike a covenant, *berîth*, διαθήκη, *foedus*,[10] which however the text does not explicitly link with the token given by Abraham as proof of ownership. The redactor provides us us with an alternate etymology of Beersheba, namely the "well of the oath", *shebû' ah*, ὅρκος, *iuramentum*, which both Abraham and Abimelech had sworn.

The interest of these popular etymologies offered by the biblical authors is that they reflect religious values of Hebrew monotheism. Of this we have a typical example in the episode of Hagar fleeing from Abraham's home where the jealousy of Sarah had made her life miserable (Gen 16:1-15). As she wandered in the Negeb, pregnant, nearing exhaustion, the "Angel of Yahweh" appeared to her near a spring of water in the desert and announced unto her the birth of Ishmael. "And she called upon Yahweh who had spoken to her, saying: Thou art the God who seeth me, *'El-rô'ï*, . . . wherefore the well was named *be'êr la-Haï rô'ï*, well of the Living One who seeth me" (verse 14). We find here, without stretching the meaning of the text, a clear affirmation of the Providence of God who looks after his own, whatever the original name of Hagar's well or fountain may have been.[11] We may be permitted to disregard the critical restoration of the text which is made to read, after much surgery, "well of the jaw-bone of an antelope".

The notice of Genesis 21:33, at first sight a mere statement of fact, is important for the history of the sanctuary at Beersheba and its function in the religious development of Israel. "Abraham planted there a tamarisk, *'êshel'*", the sacred tree, or grove, ἄρουρα, *nemus,* of the sanctuary, "and he called on Yahweh, *'El-'Olâm*, Θεὸς αἰώνιος, *Deus aeternus,* the Everlasting God" (KJ). In fact, the Semitic *'ôlâm* ex-

---

[10] Genesis 15: 9-21 describes a covenant sacrifice by which Yahweh, who exceptionally appears as judge and party, concludes an alliance with Abraham. The victims for the sacrifice are quartered and disposed in rows; the covenanters walk ritually between them, swearing that if either one of the parties violates his oath, he will be cut into pieces like the victims.

[11] According to Genesis 16:14, the well *la-haï rô'ï* is between Kadesh (*'Aïn Qedeis*) and Béred (*'Umm el-bared*), some sixty miles south of Beersheba, on a desert track leading toward Egypt.

presses not only the idea of eternity, but of universality in time and space. *'El-'Olâm* means both the Eternal God and the God of the Universe,[12] over against a local or tribal deity; thus the covenant of Abraham with Abimelech is sealed forever by the same divine authority, which even a foreigner should acknowledge.

Beersheba had been a sanctuary of Abraham and Isaac as they sojourned in the Negeb. It figures again, with different connotations, in Genesis 46:1-5. Jacob, in his old age, ready to depart from Canaan to join his son Joseph in Egypt by the train of chariots which Pharaoh had sent, was favored by a nocturnal vision of the God of Isaac, and offered a sacrifice on the altar of Beersheba. One day his descendants would be brought back to the land of Canaan, no longer a tribe of nomdaic shepherds, but a sovereign people. Thus Beersheba would become a landmark in the history of Israel. Jacob's vision closes the patriarchal age and opens a new era, the era of conquest and settlement of the land.

We may now summarize, on the basis of the obervations gathered in the course of our reading of Genesis, what appears to be the essential elements of the Hebrew places of worship: a consecrated area, exclusive abode of the Deity, from which every profane activity is banned as sacrilegious — the *Haram* of practically all Semitic religions. It is not determined by human choice, but by God himself, who has revealed his presence to the leader by a secret inspiration or a theophany. An altar of field-stones is built, upon which sacrificial victims will be offered. The life-giving virtue of the deity animates the sacred tree or grove in whose foliage the voice of the wind delivers messages and renders oracles (cf. 2 Sam 5:23). The stone pillar, *matsêbah*, is more than the aniconic symbol of the divine presence; it is *beth 'El*, God's house, and the worshippers anoint it with oil.

A well or a spring provides the water for the service of the high place. Water is a token of God's favor in an arid country.

---

[12] The opening *Surat* of the Qoran invokes Allah as the "Lord of the worlds", *Rab il-'alamîn* (same root as the Hebrew *'ôlâm*). Cf. the clausule "world without end", in the Anglican prayer book.

There is always something mysterious in the search for locating a sheet of underground water. For the Semites, the digging of a well is a solemn, religious act. We would quote here, from the Book of Numbers (21:16-17), the following fragment from an old hymn:

> And Israel sang this song:
> Spring up, O Well! Sing ye to it!
> The well which princes dug,
> which the nobles of the people delved
> with their scepters and with their staves.

The practice of burying prominent members of the tribe close to or in relation with the place of worship would later be frowned upon by the priests of Jerusalem, who feared the competition of country sanctuaries and regarded them indiscriminately as unorthodox or Ba'alist. But they never succeeded in uprooting popular customs, which survived even the christianization and islamization of the land, and dotted the Palestine and Jordan countryside with little chapels built over the graves or cenotaphs of some revered, and often legendary ancestors.

To attempt a motivated characterization of the religion of the Hebrew patriarchs is not within the scope of our study; what we have learned through our phenomenological survey of their sanctuaries is of itself insufficient for theological conclusions. Personally we would bluntly reject those speculations which regard the religion of the patriarchs as merely the first phase of a mechanistic evolution of the faith from tribal-local to national, to universal, and to otherworldly. The historically attested tendency of the Hebrews, clearly manifested from the very beginning of the patriarchal period, is to separate themselves from the ethnic groups surrounding them; this gives great credibility to the claims of Hebrew monotheism, in spite of affinities of expression with the phenomenology of Semitic cults, and in spite of the various names, some of them borrowed, by which they would address the deity. The same One God is in the midst of his people from generation to generation and leads them in their wanderings. It is true that the tradition was gathered, edited and written in the present form only centuries later by the scribes of the temple, who had "an ax to grind"; a certain reshaping of the primitive data was unavoidable during the long process of transmission. But the scribes could not possibly have succeeded in altering their sources in all cases; they were not forgers, and there is no forger who sooner or later will not unwittingly expose his own forgery.

At any rate there does not seem to be much of a kinship between the faith of the patriarchs and of Moses as well, and the artificial or political theology of Ikhnaton, the heretical Pharaoh (1377-1358 B.C.), in spite of romantic assertions by a few modern scholars. The religion of the patriarchs is, in essence, genuine monotheism, not an ideology.

CHAPTER TWO

The Ark and the Tabernacle

THE BURNING BUSH. The episode of the Burning Bush in Exodus 3:1-14 is the natural opening for this chapter. The mysterious theophany at the foot of Mount Sinai is unusually rich in doctrinal aspects and heavy of consequences. The voice which Moses heard was the voice of God speaking the Word, "and the Word was made flesh" (John 1:14). St. Clement of Alexandria, commenting on the bush that burned and was not consumed, had before his eyes the vision of Christ, derided by soldiers and crowned with thorns.[1] St. Gregory of Nyssa saw in the Burning Bush a figure of the Theotokos in her virginal motherhood, and found by derivation the basis for his mystical theology.[2] For the doctrine of the Logos was not for the Fathers a piece of metaphysical speculation, a philosophical theory to explain how the Transcendent could communicate with earthly finite beings, but it was the very heart of their teaching on salvation.

We shall single out two points of the divine message recorded by the biblical author which appear essential to our present objective, namely tracing the origins of the temple religion. The mysterious being who spoke to Moses out of the Burning Bush identified itself as "the God of thy father, the God of Abraham, the God of Isaac, the God of Jacob", one God whom the Patriarchs had named by means of the divine attributes commonly known or understood in the Semitic west: the Most High, *'El-'Elyôn*; the Eternal, *'El-'Olâm*; the Almighty, *'El-Shaddaï*; the Living Providence of Hagar at the well in the wilderness. This indicates unmistakably the universality of Hebrew monotheism and the continuity of a

[1] Clement of Alexandria, *Paedagogus* 2:79. P.G. 8:488.
[2] St. Gregory of Nyssa, *Vita Moysis, Theoria.* P.G. 44:332.

27

tradition running from the patriarchs to Moses and, as we shall see in the following chapters, to the age of the Israelite kingdoms and to late Judaism. The religion of Moses is not a radical innovation, nor does it mean a breaking away from the past; it is rather an authentic affirmation of those principles by which the people lived and would live through the successive phases of its existence. Accordingly, we should place ourselves at the vantage point from which the Book of Exodus in its final redaction interprets the course of divine revelation.

Moses had asked from God, as a mark of accreditation, what was his proper name. The answer had been indirect, even elusive: "I am that I am", *'ehyeh 'ashér 'éhyeh* (Ex 3:14). In the third person, "I am" becomes "He is", *Yahweh*. Here the Greek version adds a metaphysical overtone absent from the Hebrew: ὁ ὤν, "He who is". This answer to Moses sounds almost like a pass-word; yet "He is", *Yahweh*, would henceforth serve as a substitute for God's proper name, which remains unknown and unknowable. The Septuagint and the Latin Vulgate render "Yahweh" respectively by ὁ Κύριος and *Dominus,* "the Lord". In some biblical sections relating events anterior to the episode of the Burning Bush, "Yahweh" is juxtaposed to *'Elohim,* ὁ Θεός, Deus. This is due to the method of composition of the Pentateuch, starting from divergent traditions or written sources. The so-called yahwistic document supposed that the name of Yahweh had been known from the very origins of mankind; the other sources held that it was first revealed to Moses in the theophany of the Burning Bush.

God's answer to Moses' request sets in full light the theme of the divine transcendence. God spoke to Moses, but remained invisible, as he had been invisible to the patriarchs; they had been made aware of him in dreams and visions, or by his divine activity in and around them, but their experience never amounted to actually seeing God. This invisibility of God is expressed by the biblical axiom that a mortal man cannot possibly see God and live. It follows that God cannot become the object of pictorial representations, graven images or idols. Aaron's golden calf or the bulls set in some dissident sanc-

tuaries in the monarchic period are downright idolatrous or
at least extremely suspicious. Only by reason of the Incarnation do men see God, namely through the humanity of the incarnate Logos, but the divine essence they see not.

Just as men cannot see God, neither can they call him by
his proper name, for only those beings can be named whose
finite essence is perceived in opposition to others and which
are, so to speak, delimited by them. But He who is fulness of
being and from whom all essences derive by an act of his
creative will cannot possibly be measured, defined, or named
by his creature. This is why a Jew is forbidden to pronounce
the name "Yahweh", and why the four consonants *YHWH*
which form the skeleton of the name are punctuated in the
Massoretic Bible with the vowel points of *'Adônaï,* "the Lord,"
or *'Elohim,* "God", vocables which can actually be pronounced
without profanation of the Ineffable One. The radical impos-
sibility for men to know the divine essence can further be illustrated by the Islamic tradition of the 99 "beautiful names"
of Allah, which express his attributes, while the hundredth
remains inscrutable. Thus we find in the episode of the Burning
Bush the foundation of an apophatic, or negative theology,
common to the three religions issued from the biblical revelation.

The lonely spot where God had spoken from the midst of
the Burning Bush became the cradle of the Mosaic institution
but, unlike the theophanies of the patriarchal age, it was not
marked by a fixed sanctuary. The place, however, would be
re-visited by the prophet Elijah (Elias), when he fled from
the vengeance of Jezebel (1 Kings 19: 1-18). As he was near
collapsing from heat and starvation in the southern desert, a
miraculous cake of bread and a cruse of water revived him,
"and he went in the strength of that food forty days and forty
nights to Horeb, the mountain of God." [3] Hidden in a cleft
of the rock, he heard the passing of God who gave him his
mission in a new theophany: a "voice of silence" following
windstorm, thunder and fire, in which Yahweh was not. Not

[3] Horeb, another name for Mount Sinai; in the Elohist document of the
Pentateuch and the Deuteronomic literature, while the Yahwist and the priestly document use the name Sinai.

until the Christian era would the desert flourish anew. The monastery of St. Catherine and the shrine of the Burning Bush are indeed more than memorials to an Old Testament figure: what is worshipped within their walls is the very reality which the figures foreshadowed.

In the little plain *d'er-Râha*, at the foot of the holy mountain, the Israelites, welded together into a single nation, were to receive from God, through the hand of Moses, their marching orders toward the Land of Promise. They would worship at the mobile sanctuary which would be carried as they fought their way back to Canaan, during "forty years of wandering in the desert" (Num 14:33, 32:13).

The descriptions of the Mosaic sanctuary and its furnishing, as we read them in the Book of Exodus, are extremely difficult to interpret; several sources were used by the compiler — no eyewitness — who tried to combine them into a single account. But our interest here is not with a nigh impossible reconstruction on the basis of the text and of questionable archaeological parallels. We will rather focus on the theological significance of the sanctuary of Exodus, as far as it can be ascertained.

THE ARK. The essential piece of Moses' mobile sanctuary is the "ark of the covenant", which Moses was ordered to build "after the pattern, *tabnît*, τύπος, *exemplar*, that was shown to him on the mountain" (Ex 25:40), for it belongs to God alone to decide in which manner he shall be served: the conception, building and furnishing of a sanctuary are not matters left to human initiative. The description of the ark in the Book of Exodus is found in duplicate: first come the instructions given to Moses: "Thou shalt make....."; secondly, repeating God's command almost word for word, the account of the work actually executed: "And he made...."

The ark itself, *'arôn*, κιβωτός, *arca*, is basically a chest of acacia wood overlaid with gold, measuring $2\frac{1}{2} \times 1\frac{1}{2} \times 1\frac{1}{2}$ cubits, roughly $45 \times 27 \times 27$ inches, on the basis of 1 cubit $= 1\frac{1}{2}$ foot.[4] It was provided with two pairs of rings

---

[4] These units of measure, as their names indicate, are not derived from

through which would pass the bars by means of which the porters would carry the ark during the march. Functionally, the ark was interpreted by the redactor of the canonical Book of Exodus following two traditions combined into a single narrative (Ex 25:10-22, repeated 37:1-9). According to one of those traditions, which seems to reflect the special interest of the Jerusalem priesthood, the ark contained the stone tables given by God to Moses to be the legal instrument, *'êduth,* τὰ μαρτυρία, *testificatio* or *testimonium,* of God's covenant with his people. Deuteronomy 9:9 calls these "the tables of the Covenant", *lûhoth ha-berîth,* πλάκαι διαθήκης, *tabulae pacti,* hence the usual designation "ark of the Covenant". An episode recorded in 1 Sam 6:19 illustrates this function of the ark as a casket for a sacred relic or object: God will punish the sacrilegious curiosity of the people of Beth-Shé-mesh, who had dared "to look into the ark" (literal translation from the Hebrew).[5]

The other source of the description of the ark in the Book of Exodus shows less interest in what was placed in it and stresses rather its function as the visible sign of the invisible presence of God "between the two cherubim" (Ex 25:17, 18, 22). These are two supernatural figures of gold facing each other from either end of the lid and framing the transcendent deity with their extended wings. The ark may thus be considered as the throne of Yahweh "who sits (or dwells) on (or among) the cherubim", *yôshêb ha-kerubim,* ἐπι τῶν χερουβείν, *super cherubim* (Is 37:16; Ps 80:1; 99:1).[6] The *kappôreth,* from the Hebrew verbal root *k-p-r,* "to cover" is properly the lid of the ark. The Greek rendering of verse 18, ἐξ ἀμφοτέρων κλιτῶν, suggests that its shape was that of a saddle roof sloping on either side. By derivation, intensive forms of the root *k-p-r* mean "covering sins", "atoning" God's anger (cf. *yôm kippûr,* the Day of Expiation); hence

conventional standards, but from the canon of proportions of an average human body.

[5] Rather than "they had seen the ark of the Lord", a weak reading of the Latin Vulgate.

[6] The Hebrew verb *yâshab* means both "to sit" and "to dwell". We may dismiss as futile pedantry the question whether the "footstool" of God in 1 Chron 28:2 is identical with the ark as Yahweh's throne.

the translations of *kappôreth:* ἱλαστήριον, *propitiatorium,* the "mercy-seat".

The two interpretive traditions relative to the ark need not be set in opposition; the author of Exodus saw them as complementry: the seat of God's transcendent power, deadly to sinners, can be approached only by those humans whom obedience to the Law has sanctified. In these conditions, the ark becomes the palladium of the nation; God leads his own as they journey toward the Promised Land. On breaking camp, Moses would exclaim: "Rise up, Lord; let thine enemies be scattered and let them that hate thee flee from before thy face!" [7] On reaching a stopping place and resting the ark, Moses would say: "Return, O Lord, unto the myriads of Israel!" (Num 10: 35-36).

The search for parallels to the ark of the Covenant in Middle Eastern cultures has yielded little which could supplement the descriptions of Exodus. There is not the slightest piece of evidence to support a theory according to which the ark, at its origin, would have contained some idol or iconic representation of Yahwer, for which the tables of the Law would have been substituted... by the monotheistic scruple of a late compiler of the Tradition! Such speculations issue not from historical or archaeological observations but from a preconceived scheme on the religious evolution of Israel, which might rather be allowed to glide into oblivion. On the other hand, it is not unnatural that the ark and its artistic decoration may show a certain similarity with some Egyptian pieces of sacred furniture such as caskets for sacred objects, or as ornate processional thrones or litters; we must however keep in mind that the descriptions of the Mosaic sanctuary are by no means eye-witness accounts which could be immediately transcribed into drawing.

THE TABERNACLE. The so-called "tabernacle" of Moses, from the Latin *tabernaculum,* is the portable structure

---

[7] Compare with Psalm 68:1 "Let God arise, let his enemies be scattered, let those who hate him flee before his face!" as we sing in the paschal liturgy. In Latin monastic usage, these same verses are recited by the acolytes who sprinkle the cells with holy water after the Sunday High Mass.

which sheltered the ark in the camp. Together with the altar, table, and other furnishings of the sanctuary, it is described at length in the Book of Exodus, whose account shows forth the same complexity and poses the same critical problems as the description of the ark itself. The technical terms of uncertain or unknown etymology in the Hebrew text and their rendering in the versions make nigh hopeless all attempts as figuring out what the tabernacle looked like; a large measure of scepticism regarding most of the reconstructions found in Biblical handbooks and encyclopedias is advisable. The drawn-out descriptions of the ornamentation of the tabernacle and of its furnishing by the author of Exodus show forth a deliberate effort at stressing the magnificence of the Mosaic sanctuary, just as the author of Kings magnifies the splendor of Solomon's temple, with little concern for historical realism: the "house" of a transcendent God must exceed whatever can be dreamed of by man, and this is but another way of expressing the theological principle that every thing in relation with the cult must be done as God himself has revealed it should.

The description of the tabernacle shows traces of two original traditions merged into a single account. Two names are given to the tabernacle, corresponding to two different conceptions of its function in the religion of Israel. First, it is called the "dwelling", *mishkân*, from the root *sh-k-n*. It is God's abode on earth, and the doctrinal emphasis is on the Presence, materialized and so to speak sacramentalized in the ark of the covenant. It somehow corresponds to Jacob's *beth-'El*, the "House of God", and as long as Israel is not definitely settled in Canaan, God's house is not a house of stones, but the tent, *'ôhél*, σκηνή,[8] which is carried from station to station while the people is on the march.

The other name given to the tabernacle is the *'ôhél mô'êd*, literally the "tent of meeting", namely Israel's meeting with Yahweh at the entrance of his house.[9] Thus Exodus 29:43,

---

[8] Arab nomads refer to their tent as *beth-sha 'ar*, a "house of goat's hair".

[9] G. Dossin, *La pâleur d'Enkidu* (Louvain, 1931), compares l'*ôhél mô 'êd* with the Assyrian *bît emûtim*, in which the gods congregate to determine what is going to pass during the year ahead. On the other hand it seems normal that Moses' advisers should assemble before Yahweh to take important decisions.

"I shall be met there, *nô'adhti*, by the sons of Israel"; cf. the Greek τάξομαι, "I shall fix them a rendez-vous", and the imprecise rendering of the Latin *praecipiam*, "I shall instruct, admonish them". The people will come to the tabernacle for consulting Yahweh, "every one that seeks him" (Ex. 33:7). The Latin word itself connotes this oracular function: in ancient Rome, the *tabernaculum* was the blind in a secluded spot of the Campania from whence the augurs watched the flight of birds in order to determine favorable days on which public affairs might be conducted. The tent of meeting, *'ôhél mô'êd*, and the dwelling, *mishkân*, are not two different structures, but alternate designations which the ancient versions combine and which figure in parallelism in Exodus 40:34; when the sanctuary was consecrated and when Yahweh took possession, "the cloud hid the tent, and the glory filled the dwelling."

The Biblical text, in its description of the tabernacle, combines the memory of the tent carried during "the forty years in the desert", with the conception of an elaborate framework on which "curtains" of linen and woven goats' hair were stretched. Discounting this harmonization, one might think tentatively of a rectangular tent shaped like the saddlle-roof of a gabled house, raised on a row of wooden posts and made fast by means of ropes and stakes. As it is described in the chapter 26 of Exodus, it does not suggest any similarity to Isaiah's symbolic tent (Is 54:2), which is the typical tent of a wealthy Arab sheikh, with its façade developed in length and the various apartments, central common room and the rooms for guests, distributed from right to left. The tabernacle is entered from one end of the oblong rectangle. The inner space is organized in depth, from front to back. The tent proper is an assemblage of ten pieces of richly embroidered linen measuring each 28×4 cubits (ca. 42×6 feet) sewn together along their edges, so as to form one continuous piece of material. A slightly larger outer tent similarly assembled out of eleven pieces of woven goats' hair measuring each 30×4 cubits (ca. 45×6 feet), covers the linen tent, the excess material providing ample protection against the elements on the four sides of the tabernacle. In addition to the double tent, the text of Exodus mentions a further layer of rams' skins dyed red, and a covering of tanned skins of porpoises, *tehâshim*,[10] presumably above the Holy of Holies, where the ark is deposited, as it will be in the *debîr* of Solomon's temple. A veil, *pârôketh*, καταπέτασμα, *velum*, divides the tabernacle into two parts: from front to back, the "Holy", *ha-qôdesh*, and the "Holy of Holies", *qôdesh ha-qodâshim*, whose access is strictly forbidden to the profane.

The other tradition which the redactor of Exodus combines with that of the tent-sanctuary conceives the tabernacle as essentially a rigid structure of wooden planks and frames which had to be assembled at each station of the journey by those in charge of the sacred things. The linen curtains previously described lined the interior, and the outer tent of woven goat's hair was stretched over it, together with the covers of leather.

Whether a tent or a "prefabricated" shelter, the tabernacle was erected in the center of a rectangular court, *hâtsêr*, αὐλή, *atrium*, fenced by a barrier of canvas stretched on wooden posts, measuring 100×50 cubits (ca. 150×75 feet). It corresponds to the sacred area surrounding the holy places of the patriarchs, and to the courtyard, or courtyards, of the temple of Jerusalem. The figures quoted in Exodus, together with the measurements of the double tent, have every appearance of being realistic. However, the harmonizing of sources in the actual text of Exodus makes a scaled reconstruction of the entire sanctuary as a whole extremely problematic, if not impossible; nor can any reliable conclusion be drawn from a mathematical analysis of miscellaneous figures given in the text, or from the numbering of posts, hooks, eyelets, loops, and miscellaneous hardware. What the Book of Exodus records is definitely not the memoir of the tentmaker or of the master-carpenter who worked on Moses' "blueprints", any more than the description of the temple of Jerusalem in the Book of Kings is the list of specifications for Solomon's architect.

The description of the tabernacle and its furnishing, es-

---

[10] The equation *tehâshim* = "porpoises" is hypothetical. These animals abound in the Red Sea. KJ "badgers" is a bad guess: the badger was considered as impure! Septuagint and the Latin Vulgate read: "hyacinth-dyed skins".

pecially if one insists on a literal interpretation of the text, poses a serious problem from the sheer point of view of logistics. A simple tent, the ark and the various pieces of sacred furniture could have been transported, if not easily, at least without insurmountable difficulty. But was the assemblage of beams, boards and bases described in the text possible at all in the desert? We may doubt it: suitable timber would have to be felled, cut to measure, pared, the joints by tenon and mortise carefully prepared, and the prefabricated sanctuary was supposed to be carried from the Sinai to Canaan by a devious, trackless itinerary through generally hostile land, assembled and dissassembled at each step of the journey.

If we consider that the compiler was not an eyewitness, but that he worked on oral traditions and sources presumably not anterior to the grand period of the Israel monarchy, it is not abnormal that his magnification of the Mosaic sanctuary may have been inspired by the actual spectacle of the temple of Jerusalem. The tabernacle ought not to have been less worthy of Yahweh than the royal sanctuary. If so, it is not the description of the tabernacle which guided the architect of Solomon; rather the reverse is true, as if the description of the temple in Kings had been transposed to fit the Mosaic sanctuary, in the absence of a sufficient documentation regarding its structure, ornamentation, and furnishing. Thus, instead of the stone-cutters and masons of Solomon, we hear of the tent-makers and carpenters of Moses, the plan, rationale and divisions of the House of Yahweh remaining similar. The mention of rings and poles by means of which the Levites carried the ark, are tell-tale. The altar of burnt-offerings, made of acacia-wood — highly combustible! — with a grille, fire-box and ashpans of bronze, was so equipped, according to Exodus 27:1-8; so also the altar for burning incense, and the table of show bread (Ex 25:23-30), on which the twelve cakes of the weekly offering, *léhem pânim*, literally the "bread of the face", ἄρτος ἐνώπιος, *panes propositionis*, were disposed in prescribed order, like the "ranks" of the *prosphorai* on our table of prothesis. The Exodus records describe also the *menôrah*, a seven-branched lamp-stand,[11] the one we see sculptured on the façades of the synagogues; the *kiyyôr*, a vat of bronze for the ablutions of Aaron and his sons, and various accessories for the service of the altars. Of all these fixtures, the altar of burnt-offerings was of course the least susceptible of being made mobile. The altars of the patriarchs had been of field-stones, and another ruling (Ex 20:24-25, cf. Deut 27:6) prescribed that the altar of burnt-offerings be built out of rough stones, as could be found on the spot — never much of a problem on the route of Israel's migration.

There is no lack of parallels to the tabernacle of Moses in some pre-Islamic institutions and in some customs of Arab nomadic tribes. Palmyrenian inscriptions of the first century of our era mention the *qubbah* which figures on some reliefs; it is a small tent of red leather, containing sacred objects, and carried on a richly harnessed camel during religious processions or when the tribesmen went to war. This usage survives, or survived until recently, in the caravan of the *mahmal* of the Mekka pilgrims, a tabernacle of precious rugs containing an exemplar of the Qoran, and in the *'otfa* or *dollah* of the Bedouins of Moab and Midian, a sort of cradle, strapped to the saddle of a racing camel mounted by a girl of a leading family, whose fiery exhortations extolled the valor of the fighting tribesmen, like Miriam the prophetess when she took her timbrel to lead the choirs of Israel (Ex 15:20). Such analogies, valid to a certain point as illustrations, remain unspecific with regard to the dogmatic core of the Biblical narrative, which records usages common to the ancient Semitic religions but transposes them radically in function of the faith of Israel.

CONQUEST AND SETTLEMENT. The divine presence had been with the people throughout their journey. "A cloud of Yahweh was upon the tabernacle by day and fire by night," and the lifting of those supernatural phenomena gave the signal for breaking camp (Ex 40:38; Num 9:15-23). The crossing

---

[11] The golden candelabrum, *menôrah*, with its seven branches, does not figure in the description of Solomon's temple, which mentions instead ten golden candlesticks (1 Kings 7:49).

of the Jordan brought the exodus of the Israelites to an end. A landslide upstream had interrupted the flow of the river (Jos 3:14-17),[12] and they marched on firm ground through the dried up river bed, as they had marched through the Red Sea. That providential occurrence was hailed by the Psalmist as he sang: "What was it, O Jordan, that made thee turn back?" (Ps 114:5). They camped at Gilgal, some 2½ miles from the bank of the river. Gilgal, possibly a pre-Israelite sanctuary, was named for a circle of stones (rad. *g-l-l*), which a local tradition interpreted later as the slabs on which the porters of the ark had stood in the middle of the river bed while the people was passing by (Jos 4:9, 20-24).

The author of Joshua tells the story of the conquest in the grand manner of a chanson-de-geste. The conquest is Yahweh's own undertaking, his conquest. On the eve of the siege of Jericho, a mysterious sword-bearer appears, challenged by Joshua: "Friend of foe?" He is the captain of Yahweh's host (Jos 5:13-15). Jericho falls as the ark is carried around the walls to the sound of trumpets (chapters 7-8). The fall of 'Aï, on the path ascending from the valley of Jordan to the region of Bethel, opens the highlands to the Israelites, who defeat a coalition of Amorite chieftains encamped at Gibeon. A second campaign breaks the power of the league of "kings" of the northern city-states, "a countless multitude of horses and war-chariots". There is in these narratives a good deal of schematization; in fact several passages suggest rather that a number of separate actions had taken place, launched by small detachments of Israelites or their allies, like the clansmen of Caleb, who fought their way independently into the south of Judah.

The settlement brought about radical changes in the sociological setup of the people, whose migrating tribes became territorial districts conditioned by geographic factors: regional decentralization, communications, productivity, and the like. The change was not without danger for the national

---

[12] According to Arab historians, a similar landslide was witnessed by workers engaged in the repair of a Jordan bridge. It damned up the river during several hours during the night of December 7-8, A.D. 1267. Cf. Abel, *Géographie de la Palestine*, I, p. 481.

consciousness and the purity of the faith. The Israelites would be exposed to the temptation of adopting the way of life of the sedentary populations of Canaan, which they had overrun but not uprooted. The listing of the cities whose inhabitants they could not drive out is impressive: "Neither did Manasseh dispossess the inhabitants of Beth-she'an and her towns, nor of Ta'annak and her towns, nor the inhabitants of Dôr. . . . nor of Yible'am. . . . nor of Megiddo. . . . Neither did Ephraïm dispossess the people of Kitrôn," and so forth (Judges 1:27ff). Obviously, the days were not yet when Israel could impose its supremacy over the land; this was the time for coexistence, and not always a peaceful one at that.

A listing of local places of worship actually frequented by the Israelites following the conquest would show how deep the process of acculturation which took place affected their religious life. Contrary to what one might have expected, the old sanctuaries of the patriarchs were not necessarily among those mostly visited. For the author of Joshua, Bethel is a mere landmark for the delimitation of the tribes of Ephraïm and Benjamin (Jos 16:1-2; 18:12-13). Judges 1:22-26 makes it a strategic site whose capture by the Israelites gave them a solid foothold in the highlands;[13] but no reference is made to the memory of Jacob, of his dream, and of the stone monuments he erected as a visible sign of God's presence. Same silence on Mamrê and the Machpelah; no allusion either to the holy places of the patriarchal age in the Negeb: Beersheba is mentioned only as a town of Simeon or as a frontier post, as Dan was in the north (Jos 19:2).

THE SHECHEM COVENANT. By contrast with other sanctuaries of the patriarchal age which have lost some of their popularity, Shechem, where Abraham had first worshipped on Canaan's soil, became the theater of a solemn reaffirmation of the Sinaitic covenant. We have a double set of fragments relative to that event: a prophetic announcement, Deuteronomy 27:2-8, whose realization is recorded in the Book

---

[13] The Book of Joshua does not even mention the conquest of Bethel. Conversely, the Book of Judges omits to record the fall of 'Aï, described at length in Jos 7:2 to 8:29.

of Joshua 8:30-35. It is strongly reminiscent of the assembly
of the Israelites at the foot of Mount Sinai. An altar of "whole
stones, on which no man has ever lifted an iron adze", was
erected. Facing the ark carried by Levitic priests, Joshua read
solemnly the entire Torah, together with the benedictions and
the maledictions on those who would violate the pact. The
summary of the assembly in the last chapter of Joshua (24:
25-28) is particularly important, in that it connects explicitly
the worship of the young nation with the religion of the patriarchs. The Law was read at the oak of Môreh, the "Revealer" (see above, ch. 1) and a stone monument was erected
in witness of the convention passed between Yahweh and his
people. We stand here on the borderline between the old
Semitic rituals and their Yahwistic reinterpretations.

Shechem would thus become the principal sanctuary of
Manasseh, the most prosperous tribe of the "House of Jacob"
on this side of the Jordan, opposite Penuel in East Manasseh, where the patriarch had been given the glorious surname of Israel after wrestling with God at the ford of the
Jabboq (Gen 32:24-32). Yet Shechem would not be the
resting place of the ark nor consequently the center of the
confederacy. The religious syncretism which had set in after
the conquest was the unavoidable consequence of Joshua letting "the people depart, every man unto his own inheritance",
into a land whose indigenous population outnumbered by far
their conquerors. While the tribes, now spread throughout
the land in their respective territories, shared with the Canaanites local places of worship without too much regard for
Mosaic orthodoxy, the sanctuary which possessed the ark
would be the religious center of the entire nation, and the
alleged presence of relics from the tabernacle of Exodus and
its furnishing would confer on the sanctuaries which claimed
to keep them an aura of legitimacy acknowledged even by
the scribes of Jerusalem who compiled the ancient traditions.

SHILOH AND THE WARS OF THE ARK. Shiloh, in
the highlands of Ephraïm, became the first sanctuary of the
nation. Archaeological soundings and surveys have confirmed
the identification of the site with the field of ruins known in

Arabic as *Khirbet Seilûn*, off the main north-south trunk road. It had been occupied by indigenous elements from the beginning of the second millenium to ca. 1600 B.C., but no clear evidence of a Canaanite city in the time of the Hebrew conquest was found. The Book of Joshua refers to Shiloh as the place where the "tent of meeting" was pitched and where the Israelites convened "before Yahweh" to draw lots in view of the distribution of territories among tribes not yet provided for (Jos 18:1; 19:51). Why Shiloh? There is in the Bible no indication of when and where Shiloh was chosen as the religious center of the confederacy. This may have occurred when the frontier between Manasseh and Ephraïm was traced, winding erratically through the woodlands and leaving ill-defined enclaves (Jos 16:9; 17:8, 16-18). It consecrated the exceptional privilege of Ephraïm, upon whose head Jacob-Israel had laid his right hand, disregarding the birthright of Manasseh, Joseph's first-born (Gen ch. 48; Jos. 17:1).

We know very little concerning the remote origins of the sanctuary. It may well have taken the place of an ancient Canaanite place of worship, just as Abraham's sanctuary at Shechem had succeeded a local cult at the oak of Môreh. But the biblical text offers no clue to such a transfer, which only an exhaustive exploration of the site might possibly establish or disprove. Shiloh is mentioned in the Book of Judges, chapter 21, as the theater of an episode related in triplicate with notable variations: the ambush of the Benjaminites in the vineyards and the abduction of the local girls celebrating with choirs and dances the "*hâg* of Yahweh", presumably the autumnal feast of tabernacles.[14]

The tent under which the ark of the covenant was sheltered is identified in Jos 18:1; 19:51, with the "tent of meeting" of Exodus, an identification which some modern critics incline to regard as doubtful, without giving their reasons. In the days of Eli, the Aaronic priest in charge of the sanctuary

---

[14] The Israelites had solemnly sworn not to give their daughters for wives to the Benjaminites thus threatened with extinction, after an internecine war between the tribes. *Hâg*, the feast par excellence, from the root *h-g-g* of uncertain meaning, perhaps "to dance in circles". Cf. the Arabic *hadj*, i.e. the pilgrimage to Mekka, so-called for the circuit around the *Qa'abah*, which is the principal rite.

under the late Judges, the tent seems to have been replaced by a permanent structure, a "house of Yahweh" (1 Sam 1:7, 24; 3:15), a true *hêkal*, as we read in the Hebrew text of 1 Samuel 3:3, ὁ ναός, the "temple of the Lord".[15]

The ark housed in Shiloh was, as in the days of the exodus and the conquest, the visible sign of the real presence of God among his people and the *palladium* of the nation. The ritual observances and the popular celebrations at the sanctuary of Shiloh had obscured the oracular element of the cult at the tabernacle. "The word of Yahweh had become rare in those days", notes the author of 1 Sam 3:1, by way of introduction to the story of Samuel and his supernatural calling. The birth and mission of Samuel were mysteriously revealed to Hannah in answer to a secret vow she had made "before Yahweh" (1 Sam 1). In the vigil of the night, the young Samuel heard the voice of God announcing the disaster about to befall Shiloh in punishment of the impiety of Hophni and Phinehas, Eli's sons, and calling him to be the charismatic leader of Israel (1 Sam 3).

The Hebrew text of 1 Sam 2:22, not reproduced in the Greek and Latin versions, mentions the presence of a group of women at the gate of the sanctuary. They correspond to the women who had given their mirrors of polished bronze to be melted for the laver of the tabernacle of Exodus (Ex 38:8).[16] In either passage, they are shown as standing guard (hebr. *ha-sôb'oth*), and it has been suggested — possibly but unconvincingly — that they formed a militia of hierodules assisting the custodians of the sanctuary. The fornication of the sons of Eli might suggest a case of ritual prostitution, not uncommon in ancient Middle East cults, but the text as it reads is rather a straight denunciation of the debauchery of Hophni and Phinehas and of their sacrilegious behavior (1 Sam 2:12-17, 22).

The retribution had begun on the spot with the defeat of

---

[15] From the Sumerian composite ideogram E-GAL, interpreted in Babylonian syllabaries as *bîtu rabu*, "the great house", the king's, or the god's, palace.

[16] The Greek text of Ex 38:8 reads: "the mirrors of the fasting ones" (τῶν νηστευσασῶν).

Israel by the Philistines in a bloody encounter on the border between 'Ebenezer and 'Aphek; the Philistines captured the ark; Hophni and Phinehas were among the slain; Eli, at the news of the disaster, fell dead; the wife of Phinehas succumbed in giving birth to a son to whom she gave on expiring the name of Ichabod, "the Inglorious", for she said, "The glory has departed from Israel, since the ark of God was taken away" (1 Sam 4).[17] The ruin of Shiloh deprived the entire nation of the visible token of God's presence, and reduced Israel to a condition which we might compare to that of a church which has been desecrated.

A detailed account of the vicissitudes of the ark from its capture by the Philistines to its transfer to Jerusalem by David is scarcely necessary. We would rather single out a few points which appear relevant unto a right understanding of God's transcendence and his universal sovereignty "over all gods", the One who is, over against those that are not. This belief finds its expression in a number of crude stories assembled by the compiler of the Books of Samuel.

The Philistines had deposited the ark in the temple of Dâgôn at Ashdôd; it was their undoing. "When they of Ashdôd arose in the morning. . . . Dâgôn had fallen upon his face to the ground before the ark of the Lord, and the head of Dâgôn and the palms of his hands were broken off on the threshold; only the trunk of Dâgôn was left to him" (1 Sam 5:3-4).[18] A plague, propagated by mice, spread through the districts of the Philistines, who were afflicted with tumors.[19] Obviously, the intention of the author was to ridicule the Philistines and their god, to the great glee of the Israelites,

[17] Ichabod, *'î kâbôd* is interpreted "No [more] glory", or "Where is [now] the glory?" whether the particle *'î* marks either a negation or an interrogation. Especially in the latter case, the "Glory", like the "Presence", is understood by the rabbis as a substitute for the not-to-be-pronounced name of God.

[18] Hebrew: "only Dâgôn was left to him". According to a hypothesis which goes back to the time of St. Jerome, the Hebrew seems to hide an untranslatable pun on the name "Dâgôn". The noun *dâg* means "fish". We may try to render the pun by: "there remained of him only the fish-part". However, there is no evidence that, unlike some deities of the Chaldaean pantheon, Dâgôn was ever represented in the Semitic west as having the body of a fish.

[19] A massoretic note of the Hebrew Bible suggests that these tumors were hemorrhoids, a sense retained by the Vulgate and the King James translators.

who needed some proof that the divine virtue had not departed from the ark, even in captivity.

The Philistines could do only one thing: get rid of the
ill-fated war trophy and send it back to the land of Israel
with peace offerings: five "graven images" of the mice and of
the tumors, one for each of the towns of the pentarchy.

The account of the home-journey is a collection of popular
stories rich in picturesque details, and otherwise not lacking a
theological significance. The stress is on the supernatural manifestations which made an invisible presence evident to all
bystanders. All along the road, the virtue radiating from the
ark inspired the same sacred terror which had overcome the
patriarchs of old at the awe-inspiring approach of Yahweh,
whose mind is inscrutable and whose will unpredictable.

Having decided to send the ark back to Israel, the Ashdô-
dites took two milk-cows "upon whom there had never been
a yoke," and separated them from their calves kept in the
stable; they hitched the cows to a cart upon which they placed
the ark and let them go freely. Instead of taking the road to
the highlands of Ephraïm, the Shiloh road, the cows headed
straight toward the hill country of Judah, lowing as they
went; "they turned neither to the right nor to the left." The
first stop was at Beth Shémésh, the first Judaean village to be
met by travellers ascending from Ashdôd in the Philistine
plain, on the border between Benjamin and Judah (Jos 15:60).
At Beth Shémésh, the men chopped the wood of the cart,
slaughtered the cows and offered them in a solemn holocaust
witnessed by the Philistine magnates. Whatever has been
used for the service of the Holy One is, by the mere fact, consecrated, and unfit for any earthly usage.

From Beth Shémésh onward, for the first time since its
abduction by the Philistines, the ark of Yahweh would be in
the hands of faithful worshippers. The next station was at
the hill of Qiriath Ye'ârim, "the forest town", also called
Qiriath Ba'al, or *Ba'alah* or *Ba'alê Yehudah*, rather unorthodox denominations from a Yahwistic point of view. Qiriath
Ye'ârim was one of the four cities of the Gabaonites, a religious league of the Canaanites whose population had been
spared by Joshua at the time of the conquest and assigned

to menial tasks "for the congregation and for the altar of the
Lord" (Joshua 9:3-27). The ark was set in the house of
Abinadab, a local worthy, and the narrator, moved by esprit
de corps and liturgical scruple — he belonged to the priestly
circles of the capital — notes that the men of Qiriath Ye'ârim
consecrated 'Eleazar, son of Abinadab, to watch over the ark
in his father's house (1 Sam 7:1-2).

According to the book, the ark remained on the hill of
Qiriath Ye'ârim for some twenty years, inexplicably unknown
to, or forgotten, by the Israelites. This chronological gap was
probably meant by the author to correspond with the years
of Samuel, the abortive royalty of Saul, David's errant youth
and his seven years of reign in Hebron prior to the conquest
of Jerusalem. Upon hearing that the ark had been recovered,
or discovered, at Qiriath Ye'ârim: "We found it in the field
of Ya'ar" (Ps 132:6), the king decided to have it transferred
to his new capital. This would be the last leg of the journey,
accidentally marred by the tragic death of 'Uzzah, 'Eleazar's
brother, smitten for having put his hand to the sacred ark in
order to support it, for the oxen pulling the cart on which it
had been placed stumbled, "and the place is called Perets
'Uzzah to this day", that is to say, "the breaking forth [of
Yahweh's anger] upon 'Uzzah" (2 Sam 6:6-8). This is one
more instance of the unapproachable sacredness of Yahweh,
believed to be physically present in the ark. We may recall
here how the Book of Exodus describes the rings and bars by
means of which the ark was carried, lest human hands come
in contact with the divine (Ex 25:26-28).

The transfer of the ark of the covenant to Jerusalem opened
a new phase in the history of Israel, an age of intensive institu-
tionalization, political and religious, with its inherent dan-
gers: in the midst of a growing prosperity brough about by
the coherent policies of the kings, the prophets had to denounce political and social abuses and religious formalism; the
tension between their religion of moral Yahwism and the
religion of the priests — a polarization, not a contradiction —
would never be resolved until the coming of Him who, as a
man, was Priest, Prophet, and King.

CHAPTER THREE

The Temples of Jerusalem

THE ARK IN ZION. The eclipse of the cult of the ark following the destruction of Shiloh, the downfall of the house of Eli and the defeat of Israel at the hand of the Philistines coincides with a period of tribal rivalries, the chaotic reign of Saul and the early years of David the outlaw. The traditions and documents compiled by the author of the Books of Samuel are not easily reconciled.[1] The number of twenty years during which the ark was kept on the hill of Qiriath Ye'ârim results from a conventional reckoning similar to the symbolic chronology of the Book of Judges: twenty years are one half of David's regnal years: seven in Hebron and thirty-three in Jerusalem. We may assume that the "invention" of the ark at Qiriath Ye'ârim, a not unfriendly place but, after all, a foreign locality, did not happen immediately after the conquest of Jerusalem over the Jebusites. The most urgent task had been to organize the defenses of the city (2 Sam 5:9). The king had established his residence in the "City of David", a rocky spur between the valley of the Qidrôn and the ravine later called the valley of the Tyropoeon. When he felt reasonably secure in his capital, he ordered the ark to be brought from the house of 'Obedédom in the western suburbs of the city, where it had been provisionally deposited. David's wife Mikal watched the procession from a window of the house (2 Sam 6:16). The solemn deposition of the ark "in its place, in the midst of the tent which David had pitched for it" (2 Sam 6:17, cf. 1 Chron

---

[1] The mosaic tradition is particularly sensible in the story of the election and anointing of Saul, in which the compiler has tried, not too successfully, to harmonize his sources (1 Sam ch. 8-10) and in the diverse fragments grouped together at the end of the second Book of Samuel, ch. 21-24.

16:1), can be regarded as the first chapter of the history of
the temple.

The tent which David pitched for the ark was meant only
as a provisional shelter; it was not the tabernacle of Moses,
the *'ôhél mô'éd* which, according to a tradition recorded in
1 Chron. 16:39, 21:39 and 2 Chron. 1:3-6 (cf. ch. 2), was
kept together with the bronze altar of the Mosaic sanctuary
at the high-place of Gibeon, the revered center of a religious
federation of four towns assimilated by the Israelites but re-
taining their own individuality. Qiriath-Ye'ârim was one of
them, but neither Qiriath-Ye'ârim nor Gibeon could possibly
aspire to becoming the religious capital of Israel, even though
the former had been sanctified by the presence of the ark, and
the latter hallowed by Solomon's vision, prayer and sacrifices
(1 Kings 3:4-15; 2 Chron 1:3-12). Both places belonged in
a pre-temple phase of Yahwism.

The place selected for the establishment of the sanctuary
was the rocky esplanade north of the city — "Zion, heart of
the North" (Ps 48:2) — where the Jebusites had their threshing floors. This was no arbitrary choice, but Yahweh's
own will, signified to David by the prophet Gad: "Go up,
rear an altar to Yahweh on the threshing floor of 'Araunah
the Jebusite!" (2 Sam 24:18 ff and 1 Chron 21:18 ff, where
the name is spelled 'Ornân). The purchase of the area is
vividly described in both narratives. The scenario is reminiscent of Abraham's acquisition of the cave of Machpelah from
'Ephrôn the Hittite (Gen 23:3-20). Buyer and seller rivalize
in generosity; David will not accept a gift, but pay a just price
fixed at fifty silver shekels or, according to the Chronicler,
"six hundred gold shekels!" 'Araunah offers his oxen, the
yokes and the threshing sledge for the burnt-offering. We
may recall here the Beth Shémésh holocaust of the cows which
pulled the cart of the ark (1 Sam 6:14) or, in another context,
the story of Elisha, called by God from behind the plough,
who slaughters his oxen for a sacrificial meal (1 Kings 19:21).
This common theme suggests that something definitive, ir-
reversible, has just taken place. The religious significance of
the entire episode is obvious.

The Chronicler states categorically that the altar erected

by David was the very first element of Israel's permanent
sanctuary. Yahweh answered the king's prayer by sending
from heaven a fire which devoured the victims of the holocaust, and David exclaimed: "This is the house of Yahweh
Elohim, and this will be the altar for the burnt-offerings of
Israel" (1 Chron 21:26 and 22:1). The text of 2 Chron 3:1
is even more explicit: "The house of God shall be built" on
Mount Môriah, where Yahweh appeared to David. ... in the
place which he had prepared on the threshing floor of 'Araunah the Jebusite." The Hebrew tradition as a whole identified
the temple area of Zion with the summit of Mount Môriah,
thus linking together the episode of Abraham offering his son
(Gen 22:1-18) and the sacrificial worship of the royal
sanctuary.

It was not given to David to fulfill his desire and proceed
with the construction of the temple. "When Yahweh had
given him rest round about from all his enemies" — a pre-
carious rest indeed! — David opened his heart to Nathan the
prophet: "See here! I dwell in a house of cedar and the ark
of Yahweh is housed in tents!" (2 Sam 7:2). But Yahweh
declined the king's secret prayer. The time was not come to
engage in a long-range building program. The foundations
of the kingdom were far too shaky. Solomon acknowledged
this in the message he sent to Hiram of Tyre concerning the
project: "You know that my father David could not build
a house unto the name of Yahweh his God, for wars were
about him on every side, until Yahweh put them under the
soles of his feet" (1 Kings 5:3). David had been called to
build a dynasty which would endure, but he used deceit, violence and blood for blood in dealing with his open or his
covert enemies, and he was denied the privilege of edifying
God's house by the seer Gad who, in the name of Yahweh,
had commanded him to build the altar of the future sanctuary.
Another charge against David leaves us puzzled at first; a
census of the people, ordered by the king at the instigation of
Satan (1 Chron 21:1-6),[2] was held to be a grievous sin, for

[2] In the parallel narrative of 2 Sam 24:1, it is Yahweh himself, apparently
angered against his people for the inhuman treatment of the descendents of
Saul, who tempts David into having the census taken, a trespass for which

Yahweh is the sole master of the increase of the people and its defense against the enemies; the prophets as a whole would always protest against whatever appeared to them as an encroachment of royal power over the pure theocratic ideal of the Mosaic institution. David's trespass was declared the cause of a plague visited upon the people and for which the sacrifices he offered on the new altar might possibly atone (2 Sam 24:21, 25).

The nostalgia of the prophets for the simple religion of the days in the desert, and their distrust of elaborate rituals appear in 2 Sam 7:5-17. Nathan, the prophet who had recently castigated David's adultery with Bathsheba' and his treacherous behavior toward the deceived husband, objected forcefully to the king taking the initiative of building the temple: "Shalt thou, says Yahweh, build a house for me to dwell in, who have not dwelt in any house since the time that I brought up the Israelites out of Egypt even to this day; but I have journeyed in a tent and tabernacle." Nathan's words echo the oracle of Amos 5:25, "Did you bring me sacrifices and offerings during the forty years in the wilderness, House of Israel?" Anyway, which house built by hands could possibly contain him "whom heaven and the heaven's heaven cannot contain?" (1 Kings 8:27; Is 66:1).

THE TEMPLE OF SOLOMON. Our information concerning the construction of the temple is drawn primarily from the narratives of 1 Kings, reproduced in part by the Chronicler. It is generally agreed that the original documents or sources are roughly contemporaneous with the monument, and reflect the impressions of an eye-witness. It is clear, however, that the description as we read it aims not at architectural precision, but rather at the edification of future readers invited to remember with awe the glory of Solomon's marvel. It abounds in technical terms, and later copyists have surcharged the text with comments of their own which add to the difficulty of interpretation. Analogies of plan and details of

the people would be visited by the plague. The more developed theology of the Chronicler introduces Satan as the secundary agent inducing the people into sin, by permission of the First Cause.

construction with ancient temples of the Near and Middle East, especially in the Syro-Phenician area, are valid, but too general to be of much help for an archaeological reconstruction.

The little we know of the post-exilic sanctuary rebuilt on the ruins of the first temple, or the descriptions of the Herodian temple, the one which Jesus visited, may be used with caution to supplement the old narratives. Their relative validity derives less from the permanence of building techniques or architectural formulae, than from their being rooted in tradition: Yahweh himself had revealed what his earthly dwelling should be, and his decisions were deemed unalterable. Whenever it came to restorations, new gates and courtyards might be added, but the "house" itself might not be changed; it was a matter of dogma, not of style.

The descriptions of the temple in Kings and Chronicles have been composed after a pattern common to the religious literatures of the Near and Middle East, which show forth an intense feeling of reverence for the sacral character of shrines and temples, going far beyond their archaeological significance. The theme is developed as follows:

1. *Divine calling of the chosen builder.* Gu-de-a, ruler of the city-state of Lagash in southern Mesopotamia (toward 2200 B.C.) is ordered by *Nin-gir-su* his God to build a temple to his name.[3] Yahweh had called Moses "on the mountain" where he would receive instructions for building the tabernacle (Ex 24:1 and 12). David's initiative of building a solid structure to house the ark of the covenant was rejected, this honor being reserved for Solomon, who was favored with a divine revelation, in order that he might provide Yahweh with a suitable dwelling in the midst of Israel; we are given to understand that the wisdom imparted to Solomon made him not only a just and enlightened despot, but also a genial and inspired master builder (1 Kings 3:4-15; 2 Chron 1:7-13).

2. *Divine instructions and description of the future temple.* Yahweh had shown to Moses, "on the mountain", a model of

[3] François Thureau-Dangin, *Les inscriptions de Sumer et d'Accad* (Paris, 1905), pp. 135-198. Excerpts (in English) in Pritchard, *Near Eastern Texts.*

the tabernacle (Ex 25:9) and given him a full description
and the measurements of all the furnishings (Ex 25:10-40).
According to 1 Chron 28:19, instructions written "of God's
own hand were handed down by David to Solomon, to make
him understand the model" of the temple and all its appointments.[4] In the vision of Ezekiel (40:3), a supernatural being
is sent "whose appearance was like unto brass, holding a line
of flax and a measuring reed in his hand", for the unity of
measure of a temple is not to be determined by humans; it is
God-given, and the weights and measures of the market-place,
loosely regulated and subject to variations, may not be used.
The temple cubit is "according to the ancient measure"
(2 Chron 3:3, hebr.), and Ezekiel's measuring reed would
be "six cubits long by the cubit, and an handbreath" (Ezek
40:5), by which we are given to understand that the sacred
cubit was to be $1+1/6$ of the current measure; note that the
prophet did not mean to innovate in any way, but rather to
restore an ancient standard, which had been allowed to de-
teriorate in daily usage.[5] Ezekiel's mysterious surveyor is a
twin brother to the divine being of *Gu-de-a*'s nocturnal
visitor, "whose stature was as high as the heavens, his feet
as low as the earth", and who brought to the Chaldaeans the
model of the temple and the standard of the cubit with its
subdivisions engraved on the statues of the king.

3. *Advanced preparations.* Moses had received contribu-
tions from all the people for the construction and furnishing
of the tabernacle, for the vestments of Aaron and his sons,
and for the celebration of the cult (Ex 25:1-7; 35:5-9 and
20-29). The Chronicler records similar collections being taken
by David: building stones, timber, precious metals and jewels
stored in anticipation of the building of God's house (1 Chron
22:2-5; 29:2-9).

Yahweh himself had chosen the skilled workers and art-

---

[4] The Hebrew text seems to have undergone some revision at the hand of
glossators. The general meaning is clear: there shall be no tampering with the
revealed model and the sacred standard of measurement.

[5] Theoretically, and according to etymology, the cubit is the length of the
human forearm measured from the elbow to the tip of the middle finger.
Cf. G. Barrois, *Manuel d'archéologie biblique* II, p. 244-246.

ists who would build and decorate the tabernacle: "Betsal'el, of the tribe of Judah, whom I have filled with a divine spirit, wisdom, discernment and knowledge in every craft. . . . I have appointed 'Aholiab to second him, and in the heart of all wise-in-heart I have put wisdom, that they do all which I commanded thee [Moses] to do" (Ex 31:1-6); art is a God-given charism, akin to the gift of prophecy, and this is why the prostitution of his art by the maker of idols is a particularly heinous sin. The authors of Kings and Chronicles describe the appointment of the architects, decorators, and master craftsmen of the temple in a similar vein. They record the correspondance between Solomon and Hiram of Tyre for the procurement of timber from Lebanon, the hiring of laborers and mariners who would fell the trees in the mountain and transport them by sea to the coast of Palestine, and of the stone-cutters who would quarry choice blocks and dress them for the royal constructions (1 Kings 5:2-18; 2 Chron 2:3-16). Another Hiram (or Hûrâm-'Abi), also a Tyrian, born to a widow of the tribe of Nephtali, would establish a foundry for the bronze utensils of the temple in the district of the Jordan, between Succoth and Tsartân (or Tserêdah). He is said to have been equally skilled in the art of the gold or silversmith and in the weaving of every kind of brocades (1 Kings 7:13-14, 46; 2 Chron 2:13-14; 4:17-18).

4. *Construction.* This section, as well as the preceding, is of course absent from Ezekiel's description of the ideal temple, which he saw in a vision, but which would not be realized. When, as in Exodus, an advanced description of the sanctuary is given by God to the prospective builder, the recording of the actual construction work follows almost word for word the text of section 2; instead of verbs in the imperative or second person of the future, "thou shalt make. . .", we read: "and he made . . .". The Chronicler reproduces, except for insignificant details, the text of the redactor of Kings, who had based his work on the tradition of the royal secretaries, while the distinctive accent of Chronicles is decidedly that of the temple scribes.

5. *Enthronement and theophany.* The old Sumerian texts relate how the divine effigies of *Nin-gir-su* and his retinue had

been installed in the house which the *pa-te-si* of Lagash had built for them and how their enthronement had been marked by awe-inspiring portents. In the chapter 40 of Exodus, we read how, on orders from Yahweh, Moses had erected the tabernacle, placed the "testimony" into the ark, set the "mercy-seat" upon the ark, and brought the ark into the tabernacle (verses 20-21). The reality of the sacramental presence of Yahweh in the tabernacle was manifested by "the cloud", *hé-'ânân,* which covered up the tent, and the "glory", *kâbôd,* which filled the tabernacle, so that Moses could no longer enter into the tent, for it was now the earthly abode of the transcendent God (verses 34-35). The consecration of the temple is described in similar terms and is accompanied by supernatural phenomena. Already when David had sacrificed to God on the altar on Mount Môriah, a fire from heaven had devoured the holocaust (1 Chron 21-26). When the ark was brought by the priests "to its place. . . . in the Holy of Holies, underneath the wings of the cherubim. . . . the cloud filled the house of Yahweh so that the priest could not stand to minister because of the cloud, for the glory of Yahweh had filled his house" (1 Kings 8:6, 10-11 and 2 Chron 5:14). The ceremony concluded with Solomon's discourse, prayer and sacrifices, and God's own answer (1 Kings 8:12-66 and 2 Chron ch. 6 and 7).

ARCHITECTURE OF THE TEMPLE. A nomenclature of the various parts and notable features of the buildings with a few figures indicative of the general proportions are all we have to work with in view of a graphic reconstruction.[6] Essential data are lacking, namely the thickness of walls and supports,[7] the respective floor levels of the temple's main divisions, the arrangement of the façade and the roofing. The "house" is a rectangular building entered from the east, and divided inside into three parts distributed along the longitudinal axis: the *'êlâm* or *'ûlâm,* from a semitic root *'-l-m,* "to

[6] Figures vary in the Hebrew text and the versions of Kings and Chronicles, Ezekiel's figures, and the descriptions of the Herodian temple.

[7] Scanty indications of the thickness of the walls in Ezekiel may have been drawn from ancient documents not used by the authors of Kings and Chronicles. Obviously the scribes who copied or interpreted original records had their own theories about the temple's measurements.

be in front", cf. the Akkadian *ellamu*; it is described as an entrance hall, 20 cubits wide and 10 cubits deep; no indication of height in Kings; the 120 cubits of the Chronicler is simply unacceptable! We imagine the *'êlâm* as a vestibule flanked by two massive piers of masonry on either side of the entrance. From the *'êlâm* one entered into the great hall of the temple, 40 cubits long, 20 cubits wide, and 30 cubits high, which 1 Kings calls the *hêkâl*. The word is derived from the Sumerian ideogram E-GAL, interpreted in Akkadian syllabaries as *bîtu râbu*, "great house"; cf. 2 Chron 3:5, *ha-bayit ha-gâdôl*. It corresponds to the "holy place", *ha-qôdesh*, of the tabernacle. The *hêkâl* was presumably lighted by means of a clerestory. A two-leaved door in the rear wall of the *hêkâl* gave access to the *debîr*, a cubic room of 20×20×20 cubits, where the ark was deposited; it was windowless, for Yahweh willed to dwell in an impenetrable darkness (1 Kings 8:12); the Chronicler adds here an embroidered curtain (2 Chron 3:14) which corresponds to the veil (*parôketh*) of the tabernacle. The etymology of *debîr* refers possibly to the practice of consulting Yahweh present in the ark, that his "word" (*dâbâr*) be made known to the priest; hence the Latin translation of *debîr* by *oraculum* and of the King James by "the oracle". The *debîr* corresponds to the "Holy of Holies", *qôdésh ha-qodâshim*, of Exodus 26:23, the "most holy place" or "inner sanctuary" of the English versions.

The biblical texts describe complacently the ornate woodwork lining the walls of the "house", and the massive doors at the entrance of the *hêkâl* and the *debîr*, made of incorruptible wood, sculpted and gilded. The entire décor suggests a Syro-phenician origin; ivory plaques from the royal palaces of Damascus and Samaria offer good analogies; they are the products of a commercial art which drew its inspiration from Egyptian, Aegean, and Asian models.[8]

The general plan of the temple will be easily grasped by Orthodox Christians, seeing that the tripartite division of the "house" was adopted for most of our church buildings: porch or narthex, the church of the faithful and, isolated behind the

[8] G. Barrois, *Manuel d'archéologie biblique* II, pp. 440-443.

iconostasis and the veil of the royal door, the altar standing in the middle of the sanctuary. But serious difficulties arise when it comes to interpreting the Bible's description of the annex that was built "round about the temple and the oracle" (1 Kings 6:5).

It consisted in a narrow gallery running around the *hêkâl* and the *debîr*, delimited by an outer wall parallel to the temple wall at a uniform distance of 5 cubits at ground level; cedar beams connected organically the outer wall with the stone-work of the "house". This gallery isolated the sacred precincts from the profane world outside. It was partitioned into three tiers of cubicles, presumably used as storerooms for the service of the temple. A similar disposition is observed in several Egyptian monuments, for instance the Ramesseum of Thebes and the temple of Edfu. The entrance to the gallery seems to have been through the *'êlâm*, and the text of Kings mentions, by the name of *lûlim* (etymology uncertain), what seems to have been flights of steps provided for within the piers of the *'êlâm*, leading to the two upper levels of cubicles; however, the late Fr. de Vaux interpreted the *lûlim* as simple trap doors. The auxiliary structure as a whole is called in Hebrew *yâtsîa'* in the singular,, viz. "the extension, the annex"; it is also called *tselâ'oth*, a collective plural, originally the ribs of the human body, hence the sides of a building. The hypothesis of de Vaux according to which the two upper levels were late additions, after it appeared that the ground floor rooms did not suffice, is not more than plausible.[9]

Archaeologists disagree on the interpretation of the two bronze columns described in Kings and parallels or derivatives as standing in front of the entrance hall. They were given the symbolic names *Yâkin* and *Bô'az*, having religious significance: "It shall stand" or "Yahweh shall cause to stand", and "In it is strength" or "In Him, viz. Yahweh, is strength." Were they intended to support the lintel on either side of the entrance? Or were they not rather free-standing columns erected in front of the edifice? Or lamp-posts? (The

---

[9] Description of the temple buildings in R. de Vaux, *Ancient Israel* II, pp. 313ff.

latter hypothesis is unlikely.)[10] Analogies suggested with
Egyptian obelisks or Canaanite stone pillars (*matsêboth*) are
not improbable, but too vague to be conclusive.

The furnishings of the temple, corresponding to those of
the tabernacle, are described as permanent fixtures, instead of
the moveable pieces of furniture allegedly carried from station
to station during the years of the wandering. We shall list
them, starting from the Holy of Holies. The ark stood alone
in the inner sanctuary (*debîr*), containing nothing but "the
two tables of stone which Moses put there at Horeb when
Yahweh made a covenant with the Benê Israel". Mention is
made of the two long wooden poles by means of which the
ark could be carried, "and they are here to this day" (1 Kings
8:7-9). This is a precious indication for dating the composition
of the first Book of Kings, or of its sources *before* the sack of
Jerusalem by the Chaldaeans.

In the great hall (*hêkâl*) were placed ten lampstands
disposed symmetrically, five on the right and five on the left,
instead of the tabernacle's *menôrah* of seven branches. Also
in the great hall, presumably on the northern side — its location in the tabernacle of Exodus 40:22 — the table of wood
overlaid with gold (*ha-shulhân*), on which the twelve loaves
of the show-bread were renewed at each sabbath (1 Kings
7:48). The Chronicler writes (improbably!) of ten tables
(2 Chron 4:8), perhaps by analogy with the ten lampstands.
Facing the holy door of the inner sanctuary stood the golden
altar for the burning of incense (1 Kings 7:48 and 2 Chron
4:19); it is this altar from which a Seraph took the live coal
which sanctified the lips of the prophet Isaiah (Is 6:6).

The sacred area contiguous to the "house", the so-called
"inner court", *hâtsêr ha-penîmith* (1 Kings 6:36), is to be
distinguished from the "great court" surrounding the entire
temple-palace compound (1 Kings 7:12). Originally open to
all Israelites, the inner court was reserved later for the exclusive service of the altar, hence the denomination "court
of the priests" in 2 Chron 4:9. The outstanding fixture of the
inner court was the altar of burnt-offerings, standing in front

[10] The hypothesis is from W. F. Albright, cf. *Bulletin of the American
Schools of Oriental Research*, n° 85 and 88.

of the entrance to the "house". Was it the altar of stones which
David had erected on the summit of Môriah when he brought
the ark into his capital? The fact that it is not described in
1 Kings together with the other appointments of the temple
may indicate that the author thought that this was the case.
Or did Solomon order a new structure to be built, more in
harmony with the esthetics of the new buildings, as Fr. de
Vaux supposes?[11] The hypothesis is not improbable, but impossible to verify. We may imagine a cubic structure of rough
stones, according to the requirements of the ritual and, on
top of this, a moveable grill on which the offerings were
burnt. It is said that it proved to be too small for the multitude of offerings brought for the dedication of the temple.[12]
For the purification of the priests on duty at the altar, a huge
vat of bronze, of monumental proportions, rested on a pedestal formed of twelve molten figures of oxen facing, three by
three, the cardinal points (1 Kings 7:23-26; 2 Chron 4:2-5).
Its name, "the Sea" (*ha-yâm*) reflects the nomenclature of
Mesopotamian temples, where the basin or pool containing
the reserve of water, the *apsû*, was named for the primordial
ocean from which the world emerged.

The texts list ten basins of bronze, *kiyyôroth*, on top of
an equal number of "bases", *mekônoth*; these were four-pan-
elled wagons by means of which water was carried for washing the victims and wiping away traces of blood or any de-
filement, a strict necessity in the slaughter-house atmosphere
surrounding the altar (1 Kings 7:27-39; 2 Chron 4:6). The
measurements of the "Sea" and the wagons and basins, as
given in the text, are downright unrealistic; the authors cared
little about technological possibilities; their description of the
ornamentation of the temple's furnishing aimed above all at
promoting awe for the invisible Presence and at exalting the
glory of Solomon.

The texts and the topographical survey of Jerusalem leave
no doubt as to the site of the temple or, after its destruction

---

[11] *Ancient Israel* II, pp. 410-411.

[12] The Chronicler gives to the "bronze altar" the measurements of 20 ×
× 20 × 10 cubits (2 Chron. 4:1).

by the Chaldaeans and the return of the exiles, of the temple of Zerubbabel and the temple of Herod. They stood on the rocky area overlooking the "City of David" to the north. The monuments following one another in uninterrupted succession on this hallowed site bear witness, each in its own way, to the constant Judeo-Christian tradition: the altar of David on the threshing floor of 'Araunah the Jebusite, the sacred precints of the national sanctuary, a pagan temple dedicated to Zeus Olympios by the Seleucids (2 Macc 1:2), the central church of the Knights Templar under the Frankish domination, and the Dome of the Rock where, according to Islamic traditions, Mohammed was miraculously transported, that he might worship on the very spot where Abraham and Jesus had prayed. Nor is there any doubt regarding the orientation of the temple, which was entered from the east. Its precise location, however, cannot be ascertained. The Rock (*es-Sakhrah*), enshrined under the dome of the mosque, had been either the podium of the altar, or the foundation of the Holy of Holies. Both hypotheses have been discussed at length by archaeologists and balance each other about even. Fr. de Vaux inclined toward the latter, on the faith of a rabbinical tradition according to which the "stone of foundation", allegedly left visible in the Holy of Holies, was identical with the rock of Môriah.[13]

The Solomonic buildings, temple and royal palace, formed a single complex north of the triangular spur of the "City of David". The architectural ensemble, house of God and house of the king, manifest the popular trend toward the monarchic centralization observed in Israel and its neighbors toward the beginning of the first millenium B.C. But the prophets, in their nostalgic fidelity to the theocratic ideal of the old days, looked askance at the monarchic regime, which may have been a historical necessity but was surely no unmixed blessing. On the one hand the college of priests serving at the royal sanctuary acquired an authority beyond par but lost in independence what it gained in prestige. On the other hand the king was tempted to meddle in the things of the cult and usurp tradi-

[13] Concerning the site of the temple, see R. de Vaux, *Ancient Israel* II, pp. 318ff.

tional prerogatives of the priests. Thus *'Uzziah* ('Azariah) of Judah, otherwise an able monarch, listed by the Chronicler among those who "sought Yahweh", made himself guilty of a sacrilegeous trespass when he offered the incense on the golden altar, against the remonstrance of the chief priest; he was stricken with leprosy and remained in confinement "to the day of his death" (2 Chron 26:16-23; cf. 2 Kings 15:5). His grandson Ahaz ordered a new altar to be built in the inner court, on the unorthodox model of the altar which he had seen in the temple of Haddad in Damascus, and he removed the bases of the "Sea" and of the basins, possibly to reclaim the metal in payment of the tribute exacted by the Assyrian overlord (2 Kings 16:10-17; 2 Chron 28:34). Manasses erected in the temple altars to idols and a simulacrum of the female goddess (2 Kings 21:4-7; 2 Chron 33:4-7). These are but a few characteristic episodes among many. Reformer-kings, like Josaphat or Josias, were never fully successful in correcting the abuses.

The arbitrary involvement of the kings in the affairs of the cult, however, does not authorize us to describe the temple as primarily a "palatine chapel"; [14] it had been and remained to the end the national sanctuary, whose destiny was indissolubly linked with the destiny of the people and of the dynasty.

"In the eleventh year of Zedekiah king of Judah" (2 Kings 25:2), "the fifth month, the seventh day of the month, in the nineteenth year of Nebuchadnezzar king of Babylon" (July-August, 586 B.C.), the Chaldaeans stormed and sacked the capital. "They burnt the house of Yahweh and the king's house, and all the houses of Jerusalem and every magnate's house". The record of the event is found in 2 Kings 25:8-17, 2 Chron 36:18-20, and in Jeremiah 52:12-20, which draw from the same source. Precious vessels, and whatever gold and silver could be salvaged before the soldiers put the torch to the buildings, were removed and deposited in the royal treasury of Babylon. The "Sea" and the bronze columns Yakin and Bo'az at the entrance of the temple were broken into pieces

---

[14] See the critique of this unwarranted theory in *Ancient Israel* II, p. 320.

and removed to Babylon with the bronze basins and other
vases or utensils. No mention is made of the ark. Was it reduced to ashes in the general conflagration? Whatever became
of it, a phase of the religious history of Israel had come to
an end with the destruction of Solomon's temple.

THEOLOGY OF THE TEMPLE. The theology of the
temple had remained basically the same as the theology of
the tabernacle. The central dogma was the presence of Yahweh
in the midst of his people: Yahweh resides in the sanctuary,
whether it be the tabernacle of Exodus or the *debîr* of
Solomon's temple. From the earliest days onward, supernatural phenomena had made evident the reality of the Invisible. The "glory", *kâbôd*, filled the sanctuary, as it had
filled the tabernacle. But the theology of the court and of
temple circles strove toward a more refined way of expressing
God's presence in the temple. On the day of the dedication,
Solomon, according to the tradition of Kings and Chronicles,
prayed in these words: "God of Israel, ...I have built for
thee a house to dwell in, a settled place for thee to abide
forever. . . . Yet heaven and the heaven of heavens cannot
contain thee; how much less this house which I have built! . . .
But let thine eyes be open night and day toward the house
of which thou hast said: My name shall be there" (1 Kings
8:13, 27-29; 2 Chron 6:12-21). The presence is not to be con-
ceived as if God were confined in a place, nor is his power
diffused and so to speak diluted throughout the universe. Para-
doxically, the temple remains the locus and focus of divine
power: the ark of the covenant with its sacred contents is
"energized" by the Living God in a unique way; one might
conclude therefore that God's *sacramental* indwelling in the
sanctuary would end with the destruction of the temple in
586 B.C. As a matter of fact, the *debîr* of the post-exilic temple
and of the temple of Herod was empty. The faith of the Israelites in God's presence was no longer linked with anything
man-made or anything created, and the very emptiness of the
Holy of Holies would become the symbol par excellence of
God's immateriality. Already Jeremiah announcing the advent
of the messianic era in an indefinite, remote future, had

pointed to the time when the ark would be no more: "In those days, says the Lord, one shall no longer say: The ark of the covenant of Yahweh! It shall not come to mind, nor be remembered, nor missed; it shall not be made again" (Jer 3:16).[15] From these days onward, Israel would have to live on a memory and on its naked faith.

The solemn prayer for the people offered by Solomon on the day of the dedication, as we read it in the text of 1 Kings 8:22-53 and 2 Chron 6:21-31,[16] shows forth another aspect of the theology of the temple, namely the covenant relationship of the nation to God. The themes of God's indwelling in the temple and of his covenant with Israel are closely interrelated, for God himself had chosen Zion as his abode on earth, just as he had chosen Israel to be his people; the security they sought in the shadow of the temple was the security pledged unto them by the God of the covenant. It is in favor of this covenanted people that Solomon addresses God: for the Israelite accused falsely of a crime, when he swears his innocence by the altar and the temple; for the people of Israel if it is defeated in war, visited by drought, or plagued with famine or pestilence on account of its sins. The themes of inevitable retribution for unrepentant sinners and the promise of divine forgiveness for those who amend their ways are exploited here in the style and the wording of the Deuteronomy, no matter which date is ascribed to the final redaction of this book of the Bible. The prayer of the king and of the people is offered in front of the altar, here, in the temple: "They shall spread forth their hands toward this house, but Yahweh shall hear them from his dwelling place in heaven, and when he hears, he shall forgive." [17]

The benefit of the covenant is extended even "to the stranger, who is not of thy people Israel, but comes from a far-off

[15] The text of the RSV is closer to the letter and to the meaning of the Hebrew original than the rather embarrassed rendering of the KJ.

[16] The latter part of Solomon's prayer, especially 1 Kings 8:41-53 (cf. 2 Chron 6:32-39) shows traces of editorial work at the hand of copyists and of the final redactor.

[17] The custom of turning toward the temple for prayer is at the origin of the frequent orientation of ancient synagogues, of Christian church buildings, and of the Islamic *qiblah* (praying in the direction of Mekka).

country for thy name's sake". Critics tend to regard this as a post-exilic complement; we wonder whether the universalism expressed here necessarily demands such a late dating. It is in accordance with Solomon's conception of the monarchy as an empire grouping people of diverse ethnic background under the all-inclusive authority of the monarch, and granting them access to the temple and participation in its rites.

As for the petition that it please God restore his people in the eventuality of a deportation (1 Kings 8:46), it may very well be a post-exilic addition; it is not likely that Solomon would have mentioned such gloomy prospects on the triumphal day of the temple's dedication. If not post-exilic, the allusion might be to events anterior to the catastrophe of 586 B.C., such as the exchanges of populations which took place in Samaria at the hand of the Assyrians, or the partial deportations of Judaeans under the successors of Josias, the temple still standing.

THE VISION EZEKIEL. We write the *vision,* not the *temple* of Ezekiel, for it was never built; nevertheless it exerted a strong influence on the theology and architecture of the second temple. Chapters 40-42 of the Book of Ezekiel must be understood not as an advanced description or a list of specifications for an architect in charge of the reconstruction, but as the record of a prophetic revelation for the encouragement of the Jewish exiles on the banks of the river Kebar, a waterway of Babylonia. It would raise their hopes to a level far above the wildest prospects of a return to the homeland.

Ezekiel must have seen the temple of Solomon in all its splendor. Being himself a priest, son of a priest, he was well acquainted with the disposition of the buildings as well as with the detail and meaning of the ritual. This was not the case with laymen who had only visited the temple as pilgrims to attend its ceremonies from a distance, or with second-generation exiles, who knew the temple only through the reports of their elders and who had under their eyes the impressive but distressing spectacle of the temples of Babylon and the processions of the gods in the streets of the city.

Prophets had generally been critical in their appraisal not

only of individual kings but of the monarchic institution as such, in which they saw an encroachment over the rights of Yahweh. The attitude of Ezekiel is all the more significant that he belonged also to the caste of temple-priests. The temple which he saw in a vision would no longer be the seat of a royally controlled institution, but of the restored theocracy, free now from all human compromises. Ezekiel hears "one speaking out of the house of Yahweh" and saying: "Son of man, this is the place of my throne and the place of the soles of my feet, where I will dwell among the children of Israel forever. My holy name they shall no longer defile, neither they nor their kings, by their whoredom or by the carcasses of their kings" — an allusion to the royal necropolis of the city of David — "by setting their thresholds by my threshold, their doorposts near my doorposts" (Ezek 43:6-8).

The commanding idea of the entire description of the ideal temple is the absolute transcendence of God, which finds its architectural expression in the radical separation of the temple from the royal palace. The house of Yahweh shall stand within two courtyards, which are not a mere replica of the outer and inner court of the first temple, several times re-modelled or subdivided under Solomon's successors. Ezekiel's precincts have a theological significance; the worshippers will be admitted into them according to their degree of consecration: the Israelites in the larger courtyard, the inner court being reserved solely to the priests.

The entire area is a perfect square of 50×50 cubits, and the buildings, namely the "house" and its dependences, kitchens for the sacrificial meals of the priests, refectories and storage rooms, would be regularly distributed along construction lines intersecting one another at intervals of 10 cubits. Fortified gates, each one with three successive sets of massive wooden doors, would give access to the outer and inner court from the north, the east, and the south. The western wall of enclosure runs without interruption, so as to isolate the Holy of Holies from any possible contact with the city of men.

Two passages, laboriously rendered in the versions, treat respectively of the eastern gates (Ezek 44:1-3 and 46:1-3).

The outer one shall remain permanently closed, for through it the "glory of God" has entered the sanctuary (Ezek 43:2-4), and no man would dare to pass through the gateway of the Lord.[18] Access to the sacred precincts will therefore be exclusively through the north and south gates. The eastern gate of the inner court shall, however, be opened on sabbath days and new moon celebrations to allow the people assembled in the outer court to watch the holocaust and the sacrifices offered on the great altar.

In both passages, mention is made of an enigmatic personage, the *nâsî'*, the "Exalted One", the "Prince" in the English versions. He seems to be an official in charge of the secular affairs of the community. As a matter of fact Sheshbazzar, the commissioner of Cyrus, is called in Ezra 1:8 "the *nâsî'* of Judah", and several persons in post-exilic and Roman Palestine claimed the title for themselves.[19] The *nâsî'* of the visions shall stand on the threshold of the inner gate while the holocaust of the sabbath is offered on his behalf and he shall partake of a ritual meal in the gatehouse of the outer court. These regal privileges do not detract from the absolutism of the theocratic ideal; they are not meant as concessions to monarchic forms, as through nostalgic attachment to the past, but in all these passages the prophet extends his gaze beyond the horizon of the present aeon to an inscrutable future and open-ended eschatology.

Little is said of the temple's appointments and accessories, in contrast with the minute descriptions of the first temple in Kings and Chronicles; only this: the ornamentation, leonine and human cherubim facing one another symmetrically on either side of stylized palm trees, is in the traditional Assyro-Babylonian manner. The altar of burnt offerings in the inner court is described as a square three-tiered structure resembling a Babylonian multi-storied tower, *ziggurat*. The lower platform and the upper story are given symbolic names after the

---

[18] The tradition of the permanently closed eastern gate of Ezekiel's temple survives in the Islamic folklore of the walled-in "Golden Gate" of the *Haram esh-Sherîf* overlooking the ramps of the Cedron.

[19] The title *nâsî' Israel* figures on some coins minted by Simon bar Kokba, leader of the Jews during the second revolt, and of Eleazar the high priest who combined civil charges with the duties of the pontificate.

analogy of Babylonian monuments, respectively the "bosom of the earth", *khêq hâ-âréts*, and "the mountain of God", *ha-har'el* (Ezek 43:13-17).[20] These analogies, especially the giving of names having cosmic connotations, imply more than a mere substitution of the traditional Mesopotamian style and nomenclature for the Syro-Phenician art forms displayed in the temple of Solomon; they indicate a new orientation in the theological understanding of the universe and Israel's place in it. It is Ezekiel's theology, more than a mere change of style, which is going to affect the transformation of post-exilic Judaism, and to inspire the master builders of the second temple.

THE TEMPLE OF ZERUBBABEL. We know very little of the reconstruction of the temple of Jerusalem undertaken by Sheshbazzar after the decree of Cyrus permitting the return of the exiles in 538 B.C. The work was interrupted by local opposition, resumed under Darius, and completed under Zerubbabel in 525 B.C. Our sources are the record of events having taken place on the site and in the restored temple, as it is found in the Books of Ezra, Nehemia, and 1-2 Maccabees, *plus* a short fragment of Hecataeus of Abdera ca. 320 B.C.) quoted by Josephus (*Contra Apionem* 1:22, n° 198), and a second-hand description in the so-called "Letter of Aristaeas", a piece of Jewish propaganda (second century B.C.), of which sections 84-104 extoll in glowing terms, but with questionable objectivity, the glory of the monument.

According to Ezra 3:12-13 and Haggai 2:3, the prophet who had urged the reconstruction against all odds, the older men who had known the first temple were sorely disappointed by the structures rebuilt under duress by a volunteer task force using locally procured materials, a far cry from the choice timber imported from Lebanon, and the skilled stone-cutters and carpenters hired by Solomon. There were reasons enough for pessimism: the hostility of the local governor, who felt

---

[20] The English versions and the Bible of Jerusalem have treated these appellations as common nouns. Instances of cosmic symbolism are rare in the descriptions of the first temple, or are mostly imputable to late redactional work.

it was his duty to inform the "king of kings" of the situation and who requested formal instructions, and the opposition of the motley rabble left in town after the catastrophy of 586 B.C.; they had occupied the homesteads of the exiles and were in no mood to vacate them.

The first thing the returning exiles did was to build a stone altar for the daily burnt-offerings (Ezra 3:3). It is described by Hecateus of Abdera as a rectangular structure having the same measurements as the altar of Solomon according to 2 Chronicles 4:1, namely $20 \times 20 \times 10$ cubits. Then came the temple proper which, as a matter of principle, had to be the exact replica of the house of God which Solomon had built according to divine instructions. The Holy of Holies of the second temple was empty, for the ark of the covenant, destroyed in the fire or carried away by the Chaldaeans, had never been recovered or replaced. Some believed that Jeremiah had hidden it together with the tent and the altar of incense in a cave of Mount Nebo, sealing the entrance.[21] The point of the story seems to be that the cult of Yahweh should be celebrated without interruption to the end of time, no matter how the divine presence, which had been materialized in the ark, would henceforth make itself known.

If the temple buildings of the repatriates looked shabby in comparison with Solomon's magnificent structures — this could not be helped — the treasury of the temple was somehow reconstituted, partly with those pieces which had been kept at Babylon and which Cyrus ordered to be brought back to Jerusalem, partly by voluntary offerings of pious Jews (Ezra 1:6-11).

The author of 1 Maccabees 1:21-24 relates the plundering and desecration of the temple by the Syrians under Antiochus IV Epiphanes (175-164 B.C.). They carried away "the golden altar, the lampstand for the lights and all its accessories. . . . the table for the bread of the presence, the libation cups, the bowls, the golden incense burners, the curtains, the crowns and the decoration on the façade of the temple, and

---

[21] The legend is obviously an amplification of the account of the death and burial of Moses "in the land of Moab opposite Ba'alpe'or, but no man knows the place of his tomb to this day" (Deut 34:5-6).

also the hidden valuables" — eighteen hundred talents, according to 2 Maccabees 5:21. Sacrifices to Zeus Olympios, the *Ba'al-Shamêm* of Syria, were offered on the altar of burnt-offerings, and the cult of Yahweh was interrupted for three years, from December 167 to December 164 B.C., when Judas Maccabee defeated the Syrians. Then the temple was purified, a new altar of unhewn stones was erected, the buildings repaired, new vessels were made; incense was burnt on a new altar in the *hêkâl*, the lights lit anew on the *menôrah* and the show-bread placed on the table (1 Macc 4:42-59; 2 Macc 10:3-8). The dedication of the purified temple, which lasted for eight days, would henceforth be commemorated annually. It is the great winter celebration of the Jews, the *hanukkah* or feast of lights.

THE TEMPLE OF HEROD. Our principal sources of information concerning the Herodian temple are two lengthy relations by Josephus,[22] the former written shortly after the Jewish war, ca. A.D. 74-75, and the latter some twenty years later, when the author reminisced on the past of his nation. In either relation he intended to be realistic, and we should read them in the same spirit, while making some allowance for Josephus' customary exaggerations and often fanciful numerical indications. The first relation described the temple as the vital center of resistance against the Romans and stressed the strength of the foundations, the massive masonry and the fortress on the northwest angle of the esplanade, which would, so they believed, insure the inviolability of the sanctuary. The second relation was meant to impress upon future generations the grandiose achievement of Herod as a builder, rather than to provide readers with a technical architect's report.

The treatise *Middoth* of the *Mishnah*, a collection of traditions gathered during the first two Christian centuries, is not strictly speaking a description, but rather a theological interpretation of the measurements of the temple with a bent toward eschatology, but without the prophetic thrust which

---

[22] *War of the Jews*, V, 5:1-6, n° 184-226. *Antiquities of the Jews XV*, 11:1-3, n° 380-402 and 410-425.

characterizes the chapters of Ezekiel describing the temple of the future.

The archaeological investigation of the temple area yielded thus far limited results, since the temple itself had been utterly destroyed and the esplanade levelled in order to make way for the buildings of the *Haram esh-Sherîf*, the "Noble Sanctuary", third in Islam after Mekka and Medina. The efforts of the archaeologists have been concentrated on the examination of presumably Herodian foundations and the excavation of whatever remains of the ancient gates giving access to the sacred area.[23]

The community of the Jews had worshipped in the temple of Zerubbabel for some five hundred years, longer than in the temple of Solomon. In spite of miscellaneous and hasty repairs, particularly after the sacrilegious usurpation of the temple by the Syrians, a wholesale restoration was urgent when Herod the Great began to reign over a unified Palestine under the aegis of the Romans (37 B.C.). But Herod thought of something more radical. A new temple would be undertaken, worthy of the monumental constructions with which he had dotted his kingdom. This might help him in winning the favor of his Jewish subjects, yet it was not totally unobjectionable: it would unavoidably disrupt the daily service while the work was carried out. And would Herod — after all a foreigner infatuated with Hellenism, a pagan culture — have his architects conform with the liturgical requirements and the traditional ordnance of the temple once revealed unto Solomon? We may assume that the perpetual service of the altar continued uninterrupted in the court of the priests. According to Josephus, the other difficulties were also happily overcome.

The construction began in the eighteenth year of the reign (19 B.C.). The "house" (ὁ ναός) was built in record time: eighteen months. It was noticeably higher than the temple

---

[23] An up-to-date account of this exploration is not available yet, except for interim reports and technical papers not easily accessible to general readers. Parts II and III of the monumental *Jérusalem de l'Ancien Testament*, by Fr. H. Vincent and A. M. Steve (Paris, 1956), discuss in detail the archaeology of the temple and the historical evolution of the city.

of Zerubbabel but this, far from being a derogation, was deemed to restore the original proportions of the Solomonic temple. The esplanade was extended and raised to a new level; its substructions and supporting walls have been traced by the archaeologists; at least the lower courses of the so-called "Wailing Wall" on the western front are part of the Herodian precincts. Monumental stairs and gates gave access to the paved esplanade whose outer zone, the so-called "court of the Gentiles", was open to all, Jews and non-Jews. Toward the south, the "royal portico", with its triple row of columns, overlooked the ancient "City of David" at a dizzying height, notes Josephus. Along the east side, the "portico of Solomon", overlooking the slopes of the Qidrôn, is repeatedly mentioned in the New Testament (John 10:23; Acts 3:11; 5:12). Gentiles were not allowed beyond a low chancel of stone, and were warned by a trilingual inscription, in Hebrew, Greek and Latin. An inscribed slab of stone was found in 1871 and placed in the Imperial Ottoman Museum in Constantinople. The text, in Greek, may be translated as follows: "Let no foreigner enter within the chancel of the court surrounding the *hieron*. Anyone caught in the act of trespassing would be cause of his being put to death." [24] This prohibition renews in fact a former edict of Antiochus III mentioned by Josephus (Ant. XII, 3:4, n° 145).

Within the chancel, stone steps led to the platform of the sanctuary. It was divided into two successive rectangular courts lined by rows of columns and communicating with one another through rich gates. The first court was accessible to women in a state of ritual purity. The second court, or court of Israel, immediately surrounding the temple itself, was open only to male Israelites, and one more step marked the zone exclusively reserved for the priests and levites serving at the altar. The court of Israel was accessible from the north, east and south sides. A massive wall barred the western side, isolating the temple from the city. This division of the esplanade into restricted zones materialized the dream of Ezekiel and translated into architectural realities his conception

---

[24] A large fragment of a similar inscription was discovered in 1935 and is kept in the archaeological museum of Jerusalem.

of the divine transcendence and the degrees of consecration of human beings. The altar of burnt-offerings in the court of Israel, a structure of $50 \times 50 \times 15$ cubits according to Josephus, was built of rough quarry stones, in conformity with the liturgical prescriptions.

The "house" itself reproduced the threefold division of the previous temples, namely the entrance porch, *'êlâm*; the great hall, *hêkâl*; and the Holy of Holies, *debîr*. The Holy of Holies remained empty. Only the High Priest might enter it, in order to perform the rite of expiation on *Yôm Kippûr*. It was curtained off the great hall by the sumptuous veil which would split asunder when Jesus died on the cross.

The descriptions of the Mishnah add little to what we know of the Herodian temple, except for a few references to passages and accessory buildings. Numerical indications of measurements are often at variance with those given by Josephus whose arithmetic is frequently disconcerting, to say the least.

Whatever innovations there may have been in the temple of Herod lie not with the distribution and arrangement of the buildings, but rather with the decoration, the orders of architecture, the pannels of the doors and the facing of the inner walls. Josephus obviously meant to impress his readers with the lavish description of the carvings, overlays of gold, and sculptured motifs; these suggest the ornamental repertory of hellenistic decorative art: rosettes, Corinthian acanthus-leaves, vines and clusters of grapes. The figure of a golden eagle on the lintel of the entrance porch did cause some emotion among the people, and young zealots, scaling the monument, took the offensive emblem down. Either it was thought to violate the law forbidding animal representations (Deut. 4:16-17)[25] or it was regarded as a pagan symbol, like the eagle on some Ptolemaic tetradrachmas or on small bronze coins of Herod.

The construction of Herod's splendid edifice was com-

---

[25] The text of Deut 4:17, forbidding "the representation of any beast that is on earth and any bird that flies in the air", is itself an amplification of the prohibitions in the Decalogue, Ex 20:4 and Deut 5:8. Representations of animals and birds on mosaic pavements of third-century synagogues point to a more liberal interpretation of the Law.

pleted in A.D. 63. Seven years later the temple would collapse in the fire lit by the torch of a Roman soldier. Jerusalem pilgrims would no longer intone their hymns of joy at the sight of its walls but wail before the ruins of its foundations. Jesus had prophetically announced the disaster which, as a man, he did not witness. The course of his earthly life had followed the rhythm of the temple's feasts. His death and resurrection would usher in the new age.

CHAPTER FOUR

Pilgrimages and Festivals

POPULAR PILGRIMAGES. Manifestations of a supernatural presence or of a divine virtue had been at the origin
of the sanctuaries of the patriarchs and of the holy places
frequented by the tribes after their establishment in Canaan.
A number of these continued to attract pilgrims long after
the centralization of the cult in Jerusalem, in spite of the opposition of both priests and prophets. The priests of the royal
sanctuary and the post-exilic college of priests and levites saw
rural sanctuaries and pilgrimages as an infringement on what
they claimed to be their monopoly. The prophets of Yahwism,
in their nostalgia for the supposedly pure days of the desert,
denounced the superstitions, abuses and immorality which
plagued the centers of pilgrimage.

A variety of factors may explain the unequal fortunes of
these centers. Some of them were held in suspicion or downright condemned for political as well as religious reasons.
Shechem, where the Sinaitic covenant had been renewed in
the days of Joshua, was suspect to the Judaeans on account
of their tenacious prejudices against the northern tribes and
of the marked tendency of the Shechemites to separatism;
to this add the rabble of foreigners imported by the Assyrians
in executing their policy of exchange of populations in con-
quered territories, after the fall of Samaria in 721 B.C. To
quote the scoffing remarks of the woman of Sychar at the well
of Jacob, "Jews have no dealings with Samaritans" (John
4 : 9).

A formal reprobation attached to Bethel, which might have
become a place of gathering for all Israel. Was it not there
that Jacob had been favored with the mysterious revelation
of God's presence, and that he had set up a stone monument

to be *Beth-'El*, the "House of God"? But the political and religious schism of Jeroboam, no matter how it is interpreted by Old Testament exegetes, had made the site abominable to all in Jerusalem, the king's men and the priests of the temple. The eighth-century prophets who went preaching "moral Yahwism" throughout the land derided the "calves" which Jeroboam had placed in the sanctuaries of Bethel and Dan;[1] one was reminded of Aaron's "golden calf" of Sinai days, or of the symbol of the Syrian Haddad-Ba'al. Amos, the uncouth puritan of Teqoa' in the highlands of Judah,[2] stigmatized the general corruption, the oppression of the weak and defenseless by the tycoons of Samaria in virulent, insulting terms, and his message was for those of Jerusalem as well.

It may be inferred from archaeological research and extrabiblical documentary evidence that some Palestinian sites, like Mamrê-Hebron in the heart of Judah or Mount Carmel in the northern kingdom, had become active centers of pilgrimage. The identification of Mamrê with the Haram Râmet el-Khalîl may be considered as certain (see ch. 1).[3] Excavations conducted in 1925-28 have brought to light the pavement of an avenue branching eastward from the trunk road of the Judaean highlands and leading to an ancient well — the well of Abraham — and to the sacred tree, oak or terebinth. Potsherds and minor artifacts found in connection with the pavement show with probability that the paved avenue leading to the sanctuary was in service during the early times of the monarchy. Later, Herod the Great undertook to build a large enclosure to fence the entire site; uncompleted and partly destroyed, it was restored by Emperor Hadrian, A.D. 135. The

---

[1] Analogies from the ancient Middle East sugggest that the young bull of Bethel may be understood as a pedestal for the divinity, present though invisible, rather than a direct object of adoration.

[2] The mention of Beersheba in connection with Dân in Amos 5:5 and 8:14 was probably suggested by the stereotype "from Dân to Beersheba", designating the frontiers of Palestine from north to south, but nothing indicates the existence of a formal sanctuary in the Negeb under the monarchy.

[3] A. E. Mader, *Mambrie, die Ergebnisse der Ausgrabungen*, 2 vols. (1957). Since the twelfth century (at the latest), other sites were considered for the localization of the biblical Mamrê. Until recently, a venerable oak was shown to pilgrims on the grounds of the Russian hospice, on a sideroad branching out to the northwest, approximately two miles from Hebron.

foundations of a Constantinian basilica in the eastern part of the quadrangle were laid bare in the course of the exploration. Sozomen, writing in the second half of the fifth Christian century, describes the festive assemblies and the summer fair held at Mamrê, the throngs of pilgrims from all over Palestine: "Jews, because they boast of their descent from the patriarch Abraham.... Greeks, because in that place angels have appeared to men.... Christians, because he who for the salvation of mankind was born of a Virgin manifested himself to a godly man.... The place was honored as the scene of diverse exercises. Some prayed to the God of all; some called upon the angels; some poured out wine, burned incense, or presented an ox, or a he-goat, a sheep, or a cock; for they were all intent upon offering at this feast, for themselves and their neighbors, the most precious and beautiful sacrifices." [4] These sacrifices, of doubtful orthodoxy, were offered on a square altar of stone, which has been discovered in front of the basilica, toward the center of the quadrangle.

In Hebron, some three miles south of Mamrê, the tombs of the nation's ancestors became an integral part of the pilgrimage. A monumental enclosure, in Arabic the *Haram el-Khalîl*, was built by Herod to protect the cave of the Machpelah from profane intrusion. [5] In the southern part of the enclosure, a church was built over the burial cave; it was turned into a mosque after the conquest of Palestine by the Arabs, became again a church under the Frankish occupation, and is today once more in the hands of the Moslems, zealous guardians of the Haram. At ground level, cenotaphs are disposed by pairs: Abraham and Sarah, Isaac and Rebekkah, Jacob and Leah. The memory of Joseph is recalled by a cenotaph built in 1395 by Sultan Barquq, who followed a southern tradition rival to that of Shechem (see above, ch. 1).

In northern Palestine, the range of the Carmel, theater of the miracles of Elijah (Elias) the wonderworker, had the potential to become an active center of pilgrimage. Its evolu-

---

[4] *Ecclesiastical History* II, 4. Byzantine coins and remains of votive offerings were found at the bottom of the well, whose water had been rendered useless through pollution.

[5] L. H. Vincent, Maskay, and Abel, *Hébron, le Haram el-Khalîl* (Paris, 1923).

tion is somewhat similar to that of Mamrê-Hebron, except for the Herodian buildings. The mountain itself, like Mount Hermon, was regarded as divine; "Carmel", wrote Tacitus,[6] "is both the name of a mountain and of a god; there is here neither an image nor a temple, following the tradition of the ancients, but an altar and sacred awe." The promontory jutting out to the sea had always been a landmark for the mariners. It was sacred to Ba'al, the thunder god who summons rain-clouds after a scorching summer, and whose cult, favored by the kings of Israel, the "House of Omri", was never complete-ly superseded by the religion of Yahweh, even after the sacrifice offered by Elijah brought back rain and fertility to the land stricken by drought (1 Kings 18: 20-45). The moun-tain never ceased to be haunted by Ba'alist and Yahwistic prophets, ascetics and charismatics of every description, and visited by the populations of neighboring districts as well as foreigners.

The pilgrimage has continued to our own day, with features of a popular syncretism which affect even the per-sonality of Elias; he is more or less confused in popular cir-cles with St. George, under the surname of *el-Khidr*, "the ver-dant one", a supernatural being revered throughout the Middle East and credited with having power over the clouds which bring rain in due season. Tourists and pilgrims are shown the traditional site of the sacrifice, *el-Mukhraka*, at the north-eastern end of the range, overlooking a meander of the Qishôn, where the priests of Ba'al were slain (1 Kings 18:40). On a nearby slope, local people visit the *shadjarât el-arba'în*, "the trees of the forty [heroes]", viz. the forty martyrs of Sebaste, to the Christians; the forty companions of Moham-med, to the Moslems; and to the Druses, the forty imâms who will manifest themselves successively until the consummation of this age. The fortress-like monastery of the Carmelites (known in England as the "White Friars"), was built on the cape itself in 1767 and restored in 1827; the crypt of the church, a natural cave transformed in the Middle Ages into an underground chapel, is labelled today "Elias' grotto".[7]

---

[6] Tacitus, *Historiae* 2:78.
[7] The Friars, who see in the "sons of the prophets" and in early Christian

The feast of Elias is celebrated each year on July 20 by a mixed crowd of Christians, Moslems, and Druses. The vigil is spent in spontaneous acclamations, songs and dances. After the solemn Mass of the day, the pilgrims rush toward the wooden statue which stands on the altar of the crypt, in the hope that its contact will communicate something of the supernatural virtue of the wonderworker to the scarves, medals or beads which they bring. Little boys are presented at the door of the sanctuary, where a Carmelite priest tonsures their heads cross-wise, as a mark of their being devoted to "Mâr Elias" for the year ahead. The last two sites, Hebron and Mount Carmel, were totally ignored as places of pilgrimage by the authors and compilers of the Bible, who may indeed have regarded them as hallowed by the memory of Abraham and the miracles of Elijah, but who were committed to uphold Jerusalem as the only place of pilgrimage authorized, nay prescribed, by the Law, and the temple as the one sanctuary of the nation.

CENTRALIZATION OF THE CULT. The Book of Exodus admitted as legitimate the plurality of several places of worship, wherever Yahweh would manifest his presence and virtue to the leaders of the people: "In every place where I cause my name to be remembered, I will come to you and bless you" (Ex 20:24). The settling of the migrating tribes among the rural populations of Canaan following the conquest was cause of this multiplication of local sanctuaries, in sharp contrast with the rationale of desert-days religion, when the Israelites on the march gathered around the tabernacle of Moses. In a sense, the situation, according to Exodus, was reminiscent of the religion of the patriarchs, who had erected their altars at the places where God had appeared to them (see above, ch. 1).

Contrarily, the Book of Deuteronomy condemns the re-

hermits the precursors of their order, date their establishment on the cape from the medieval occupation by the Latins. In fact, there stood on the site of their church, built in 1767, an antique monastery of Greek monks, dedicated to St. Margaret, *alias* Marina or Pelagia, whom modern hagiographers regard as the feminine counterpart to St. George. See the critical study of Dr. Clemens Kopp, *Elias und Christentum auf dem Karmel* (Paderborn, 1929).

gional sanctuaries of the tribes, which however continued strong under the monarchy, in spite of the combined efforts of the kings and the temple-priests to insure the unity of Israel as a national and religious community. The scribes who compiled the book dated their narratives from the last days of Moses, placing themselves at the vantage point of the people coming in sight of Canaan across the rift of the Jordan valley, by the effect of a literary device which detracts in no way from the substance of the tradition. Accordingly, the verbs in the main passage of Deuteronomy relative to the centralization of the cult are in the future tense, and do not indicate where the national sanctuary would be located.

> You shall seek the place which the Lord your God will choose out of all your tribes to put his name and make his habitation there; thither you shall go, and thither you shall bring your burnt-offerings and your sacrifices, your tithes and the offerings that you present, your votive offerings, your freewill offerings, and the firstlings of your herd and of your flock. . . . You have not as yet come to the rest and to the inheritance which the Lord your God gives you. But when you go over the Jordan and live in the land which the Lord your God gives you to inherit, and when he gives you rest from all your enemies round about, so that you live in safety in the place which the Lord will choose to make his name dwell there, thither you shall bring all that I command you . . . .Take heed that you do not offer your burnt-offerings at every place that you see; but at the place which the Lord will choose in one of your tribes, there you shall offer your burnt offerings and there you shall do all that I am commanding you. (Deut 12:5-6, 9-11, 13-14)

The centralization of the cult in Jerusalem was not achieved until the latter phase of the Judaean kingdom,[8] due

[8] The religious policy of Josiah was inspired by the fortuitous discovery of a book of Tôrah hitherto unknown or lost (2 Kings 22:8-11; 2 Chron 34:14-19). It seems to have been a source or an early version of the canonical Deuteronomy.

to the persistence of local "high places", Yahwistic or not. The royal clergy never ceased to affirm that Jerusalem was indeed the sanctuary anonymously referred to in the deutero-nomic tradition. There, all male Israelites were commanded to appear three times a year before Yahweh, to offer their sacrifices and acquit themselves of their vows; in other words, all sacred functions requiring the assistance of a levitic priest ministering at the altar were to be performed exclusively in the temple of Jerusalem.

We are at a loss to imagine to what extent and how these exacting precepts were observed by the average Israelite. Literal compliance could hardly be expected, especially from the inhabitants of far-away districts, and became radi-cally impossible for those of the diaspora. One has to suppose that some provision was made for hardship cases or exceptional circumstances, and that some *modus vivendi* had been arrived at by tacit agreement. A few texts suggest the existence of an interpretive jurisprudence that would clarify and temper the precepts of the Law. The Deuteronomy, after stating the Law in all its rigor, admits the following mitigations: Israelites from distant regions, instead of bringing their offerings in kind, could buy the victims to be presented to the altar on the markets of Jerusalem, and partake of them in communion (Deut. 14:24-26). As for the triennial tithe, they were permitted to keep it in their own town and pay it to the Levite living nearby,[9] if the journey to the national sanctuary was too long for them (Deut. 26:12-13).

The casuistry of the Talmud, while reflecting the common usage in the late decades of the Herodian temple, is not parti-cularly illuminating, even when it lists the categories of per-sons excused from presenting themselves before the Lord on the three big festivals of the year: "a deaf-mute, an idiot or a moron, one of undefined sex (*tumtum*), a hermaphrodite, women, slaves not yet emancipated, the lame, the sick, the

[9] In Matthew 8:2-4, Mark 1:40-45, Luke 5:12-15, a leper healed by Jesus is ordered "to show himself to the priest". But which priest, if not a priest having his home in the region? The evangelists relate how the man spread the news of the miracle in the villages of Galilee, but nothing indicates that he had to go to Jerusalem for the ritual of purification prescribed by chapter 14 of the Leviticus.

aged, whoever is not able to go up on foot, a baby whom
his father could not carry pick-a-back from Jerusalem to the
Temple Mount" (Treatise *Hagigah* 2a).

THE JEWISH FESTAL CALENDAR. The calendar
elaborated by the royal scribes and still in use in the time of
Jesus for the liturgical service of the temple, combined two
modes of time-reckoning. The one was based on the natural
rhythm of seasons through the year, following the course of
the sun empirically observed; the other, on the monthly appearance of the crescent moon in the evening sky. A succession of twelve moon-cycles gives a total of roughly 354 days,
versus the average solar year of 365¼ days. This called for
adjustments in order to make up for the eleven days and six
hours of difference, ever so approximately, for there is no
easy way to reconcile the solar and lunar reckoning — witness
the purely lunar Islamic calendar, whose months revolve
throughout the solar calendar-year, with the consequence that
the months of the "First Spring", *Rebîa' el-'Awwâl*, and of
the "Second Spring", *Rebîa' et-Tâni*, can fall as well in the
torrid Arabian summer or in the heart of winter. The adjust-
ment of the lunar calendar with the solar year was made in
the ancient Middle East by adding a thirteenth month to the
year, before the first moon of spring,[10] whenever the discrepancy between lunar and solar reckoning appeared excessive,
which happened in fact every two or three years. Circumstantial evidence more than formal statements attest to the practice
of intercalation by the Israelites in the time of the monarchy
and probably even earlier. The old-fashioned empirical ways
continued after the ruin of the temple. Gamaliel II, who
presided the Sanhedrin-in-exile at Yamnia, wrote to the Jews
of the diaspora: "We let you know that the lambs are still
too young and the fowls too small; the grain is not ripe yet;
therefore we have decided, my colleagues and I, to add thirty
days to this year." [11] Not until the fourth century in our era

[10] The intercalation of a thirteenth month when needed, either in autumn
or in spring, is attested for Babylonia and Assyria since the beginning of the
second millenium.

[11] Quoted by G. Dalman, *Aramaische Dialektsproben*.

was the empirical determination of embolismic years replaced by a scientifically devised system based on a nineteen-year cycle, during which one counted seven intercalations.

Three sets of designations for the lunar months of the Hebrew calendar are found in the books of the Bible: first, names commonly used in the Phenician and Canaanite districts, Cyprus and Carthage; some of them are characteristic of seasons, several others refer to pagan ceremonies and may have proved offensive to the redactors of Kings and Chronicles. Secondly, and preferably, mere ordinal designations: first, second, third month, and so on, counting from the first moon of spring. Thirdly, during and after the Exile, the Jews adopted matter of factly the names currently used throughout the Babylonian empire, much as we use today the names of months and of weekdays without reflecting on their pagan origin. Our table shows the correspondence of the three sets. Note that the etymologies indicated are merely hypothetical; an asterisk is placed before the names of the Babylonian months *not* extant in the canonical books of the Bible but used in extra-biblical documents.

"Canaanite" months	*"Babylonian" months*	*Corresponding to:*
1 'Abîb "ears of grain"	Nîsân	March-April
2 Zîw "blossoms"	*'Iyyâr	April-May
3	Sîwân	May-June
4	*Tammûz [12]	June-July
5	*'Ab	July-August
6	'Elûl	August-September
7 'Êtânim "the flowing brooks" [13]	*Tishrî	September-October
8 Bûl "fruit" (collective)	*Marheshwân	October-November

[12] Ezekiel 8:14 mentions the "wailing for Tammûz", which took place in the fourth month (June, July) — not used as a month-name by the biblical authors.

[13] In opposition to intermittent river-beds, all dried up in that season. The etymology of *'Etânim*, the seventh month, and Bûl, the eighth month, is most uncertain.

9	Kislêw	November-December
10	Têbêth	December-January
11	*Shebât	January-February
12	'Adâr	February-March
13	we-'Adâr, i.e. "and 'Adâr" in embolismic years.	

The festal calendar of the Israelites begins in spring; hence the importance of determining accurately the first day of the moon of Nîsân. This was done by watching for the first appearance of the silvery crescent at sunset. Scientific reckoning was probably not used before the fourth century of our era; at any rate it would supplement, rather than supersede, the empirical ways retained through liturgical archaism. The Talmud discusses the procedure for verifying the reports of persons who claimed to have seen the crescent of the new moon in the evening sky; their testimony was examined by the Sanhedrin and later by a commission of three experts whose verdict was notified to the people by fire-signals lit on strategically chosen summits of the Judaean highlands, and by messengers who ran throughout the land, often without waiting for the official decision. Maimonides (Rabbi Moses, twelfth cent.) describes the procedure at length.

The new moon of Nîsân marked the opening of the sacral year. It was "New Year, Rôsh ha-shânah, for the kings and the feasts", whereas the first day in Tishrî was "New Year for the counting of years, the septennial cycle and the Jubilee, the plants and the herbs" (Mishnah, Rôsh ha-shânah I, 1), marking the passage from one agricultural cycle to the following; then is the year's harvest safely stored, the new wine pressed, and the fields left fallow until the late autumn showers and winter ploughing. In modern parlance, the first of Tishrî is simply "New Year", Rôsh ha-shânah, without further qualifications, roughly corresponding to the beginning of our church-year.

PASSOVER. The yearly cycle of feasts opened in the first spring month with the paschal solemnity. This was a complex festivity, an authoritative study of which has yet to be written.

The biblical source material consists in allusions to memorable instances of paschal celebration, in fragments of ritual and ceremonial rubrics, and in liturgical calendars. We are confronted with the vexing problem posed by traditions of diverse origin, age or purpose, collected by later compilers and editors whose aim was to record the usage of the temple as they knew it, rather than to trace critically the centuries-long evolution of the feast. It combined two distinct observances, the ritual slaughtering of a yearling lamb and the meal that followed, with the observance of the unleavened bread, the *matsoth*, ἄζυμοι. The former rite was a sacrifice offered by shepherds for the blessing of their flocks throughout the year. The latter was associated with the offering of the first handful of ears of grain, the *'ômér*, presage of the harvest which would be gathered during the succeeding weeks; accordingly, the *matsoth* symbolized the beginning of the new life-cycle, as nothing was to be left of the old baking leaven of the past year.

The Mosaic institution united the twin festivals into the week-long celebration of passover, which was made to commemorate the liberation of the Israelites from Egyptian bondage and the constitution of their tribes as a nation. The name of the feast, *pesach*, πάσχα, was explained by means of a popular etymology: the angel of death send by God to strike the first-born babes of the Egyptians "passed over" the houses of the Israelites signed with the blood of the lamb; [14] a late meal was eaten in a hurry; the matsoth would recall the bread which the women had baked without waiting for the dough to rise when the Israelites departed furtively under cover of darkness.

The "historical" allusions of the biblical narrative are clearly accessory with regard to the pastoral and agrarian ritual of the spring-lambs and the offering of the first ears of barley. This may be inferred from Exodus, chapters 7-10, *passim*, where Moses, in order to persuade Pharaoh to "let my people go", refers repeatedly to the feast which "God

---

[14] The Bible relates explicitly the legal prescriptions on the redeeming of the first-born to the episode of the Egyptian children being slain by the angel and of the Hebrew children being spared (Ex 13:15).

commanded them to keep", and to the gathering of the
people for the appointed sacrifice "in the wilderness, a three
days' journey"— a plausible argument which left Pharaoh
half-convinced, while the final outcome proved to be the
flight of his Hebrew subjects.

Passover was originaly a family festival: the head of each
household would have the lamb slaughtered and roasted at
home, and all members of the family, servants and guests in-
cluded, would partake of the passover meal. Only when the
cult began to be centralized did passover become a pilgrimage
feast, for the priests had monopolized the immolation of the
lambs. Some critics attribute this change to the religious reform
of Josiah following the "invention" of the Deuteronomy in the
temple. Such a dating seems too late. We would rather interpret the transformation of the family feast into a public
liturgy as a normal consequence of the centralization of the
cult in the national capital of David and Solomon. There is
no indication in the national capital of David and Solomon.
There is no indication in the Bible of what became of the
older practice under the new regime; it probably did not disappear altogether, even if it was frowned upon by the priests.
On the other hand, it is not unlikely that early Israelites might
have chosen, of their own accord, to assemble at some nearby
sanctuary of the tribe or clan for the feast, and the construction of the temple added to the private celebration of passover "by families" the further incentive of the Jerusalem pilgrimage. What was new in the passover of 622 B.C., a passover "such as none had been kept since the days of the Judges"
(2 Kings 23:22), is that Josiah's reform tightened the ex-
isting ritual prescriptions and aimed at ending the unsettled
condition of religious practice in Israel.

The time fixed for the immolation of the lamb was "between the two evenings", Hebrew *bên ha-'arbaïm*, a "dual"
form, meaning the time between the setting of the sun and
nightfall, on the fourteenth day of the month of *'Abîb*
(*Nîsân*) ; [15] the paschal meal would follow on the same night.

[15] The Hebrews counted the days from sunset to sunset; compare with
our Orthodox vigil beginning with Great Vespers, or with the "First Vespers"
of certain feasts in the Latin breviaries.

Two remarks are in order at this point: passover can fall on any day of the week, though it happened to be called a *sabbath*, inasmuch as the sabbatical abstention from work is prescribed for the day. Our second remark is that the observance of the unleavened bread (*matsoth*), originally distinct from the passover celebration, had become an essential feature of the paschal meal, and one would speak of "the days of passover or "the festival of *matsoth*" as synonymous.

A provision was made in the Law for a repeated celebration of passover in the second month of spring, *Zîw*, for the benefit of those Israelites prevented from partaking of the sacred meal "through touching of a dead body, or afar off on a journey" (Num 9:9-11; cf. 2 Chron 30:2-3). These dispositions became of the greatest interest for the Jews of the diaspora who wished to keep the feast according to the strict temple rules. As for the *sêder* meal of modern Judaism, it is but the ghost of the antique observance, which itself was the figure of our Christian pascha.

The complexity of the ritual and the many problems raised by the ancient Hebrews' reckoning of time gave rise to the labyrinthine casuistry of the Mishnah and of the Talmudic scholars. Unavoidable fluctuations resulted from the empiricism of astral observation, from weather conditions, or from the difficulty of communications between the various districts of Palestine. They made singularly arduous the problem of keeping in due season what was originally a pastoral and agrarian festival as well as a historical commemoration. The special problem (insoluble?) of the chronology of the last supper and of the passion of Christ will be examined in chapter 7.

PENTECOST. The second feast of the year was called the "feast of weeks", *hâg ha-shâbu'oth*, ἑορτὴ ἑβδομάδων (Ex 34:22 and Deut 16:10). It marked the completion of the grain harvest, of which the first handful of ears, the *'ômér*, had been presented to Yahweh during the week of passover--*matsoth*. Exodus 23:16 describes it as "the feast of the harvest", *hâg ha-qâtsîr*, "of the first fruit of your labor, of that which you have sown in the fields." The Pentateuch does not connect the feast of weeks with any particular event in the history of the people. Yet it was interpreted and formally acknowledged in rabbinical exegesis as a memorial of the giving of the Tôrah to Moses; some chronological notations in the Book of Exodus describing the march of the Israelites from Egypt to Mount Sinai, unfortunately marred by errors of copyists, seem to support the validity of the tradition.[16]

The festival was to be held fifty days after passover; more precisely, seven weeks *plus* one day after the offering of the ʿômér on the second day of the paschal celebrations. Thus the feast of weeks would fall on the sixth of *Siwân* (May-June) and, like passover, on any day of the week. According the opening verses of the description of the feast in Leviticus 23:15-21, "You shall count from the morrow of the sabbath. . . , counting fifty days from the morrow of the sabbath"; this was interpreted by the Pharisees to mean that abstention from work, after the manner of the periodic sabbath, was mandatory, even though the feast would fall on a normal working day. The interpretation of the Pharisees, which has prevailed in modern Judaism, was much discussed in the time of the Mishnah.[17]

The feast of weeks is one of the three annual pilgrimages which the Law made mandatory for all male Israelites (Ex 23:16-17). It was well attended in post-exilic Jerusalem. Josephus mentions "myriads" of foreign pilgrims from Galilee, Idumaea, Jericho and the Jordanian districts, together with the burghers of the capital and the villagers of the nearby countryside who could afford to leave their fields for a few days (*Antiquities* XVII 10:2, n° 254). Josephus' testimony is paralleled by St. Luke's description of the first Christian Pentecost, witnessed by a crowd of foreigners, such as haunt pilgrimage centers at all times and in all parts of the world (Acts 2:1-13). But it must have been difficult for the Israelites of distant provinces to set out on a long journey,

---

[16] See the discussion in *St. Vladimir's Theological Quarterly* 21/3 (1977), pp. 150-152.

[17] The Boethusians, a splinter group of the Sadducees, interpreted the term "sabbath" in Leviticus 23:15-16 as the first Saturday after the passover; that makes the feast of weeks automatically fall on a Sunday. See the article "Pentecost" in the *Jewish Encyclopedia*, p. 593.

while the wheat was being harvested and brought to the threshing floors, and when so much remained to be done in the gardens, orchards and vineyards. This may have prompted the priests and the temple scribes to remind the Israelites that the three annual pilgrimages, in spite of their unequal duration should be given equal status with regard to legal obligation. Thus the Talmud (*Mo'êd Qatân* 19 b) affirms that the feast of weeks is on par with passover and the feast of tabernacles, *sukkoth*, "not according to the statement of one or another of the sages"; it was not regarded as a private opinion but a *halakah* allegedly going back to Moses himself. The Levitic ritual had kept the character of the feast as a joyful thanksgiving for the harvest, with the "waving" before Yahweh of the leaves of bread, *léhem tenûphah*, made of fine flour from the new grain and baked with leaven, as an offering of first fruits, *bikkurim*. The post-exilic development of Judaism as a doctrine placed the emphasis on the spiritual joy to be derived from the study of the Law, as a sign of which house and synagogue were decorated with garlands and sprays of green foliage — compare with similar customs in Russian Orthodox churches, and the French surname of *Pâques fleuries*, "flowery Easter", for the Sunday of Pentecost. The fifty days from Pascha to Pentecost, which we count now from the night of the Resurrection, would become our Christian celebration of the new Law given to the Church, no longer the Pentecost of the Book, but the Pentecost of the Spirit whom Jesus Christ would send to his own.

THE "HIGH HOLIDAYS". In the month of *Tishrî* (September-October), a cluster of celebrations (Lev 23:23-44) signalled the closing of the agricultural year, when the olives were being crushed for oil, and the grapes brought to the rock-cut vats for pressing. Then a new cycle began; one looked forward to the first rain of the season and the winter-ploughing. On the first day of *Tishrî, Rôsh ha-shânah*, the Jewish new Year was heralded by blasts of the ram's horn, the *shôfar*. The tenth day, *Yôm Kippûr*, the day of atonement, was sanctified by fasting and prayers of repentance for the sins and transgressions of the priests and the people. Then came the feast of the tabernacles, *Sukkoth* (Lev 23:34; Deut 16:13-15). It is called ἑορτὴ τῶν σκηνῶν or τῆς σκηνο-πηγίας in the Septuagint and the New Testament (John 7:2); it is also designated as feast of the in-gathering, *ḥâg ḥâ-'âsîf* (Ex 23:16), or merely *the* feast par excellence, *hé-ḥâg* (1 Kings 8:2; 2 Chron 7:8), or feast of Yahweh (Lev 23:39; Judges 21:19). One may judge from the multiple aliases how popular the feast was. It was one of the three pilgrimages prescribed by the law of the temple. It had been originally, and continued to be, a rural festival, like the week of the unleavened bread and the day of Pentecost. The term *sukkoth*, the "tabernacles", refers to the huts of branches and foliage erected in the vineyards in the time of harvesting the grapes. The Israelites were to pass the eight days of the feast,[18] from the fifteenth to the twenty-third of Tishrî, under similar shelters. In the city they would build a *sukkah* in the courtyard or on the terrace of their house.

Leviticus 23:42-43 sets the feast in relation to the historical events of the march of the Israelites in the desert: "All that are native in Israel shall dwell in booths, that your generations learn that I made the people of Israel dwell in booths when I brought them out of the land of Egypt." Late Judaism stressed further the connection of the festival with the Sinaitic alliance by adding, on the ninth day of the celebration, the feast of the *Simbath Tôrah,* the "Rejoicing in the Law". On that day, a hymn of the synagogue similar in inspiration and wording to the hymns of the feast of weeks, sings the following verses: "The Law is the source of our strength and our light. ... With gladness and joy we sing the Lord's praises chanted by Israel, nigh unto Him who is the rock divine. ... Thrice blessed are you, Israel, that God chose you in the wilderness and gave you as his gift the heritage of the Tôrah." [19] In addition to the daily and festal sacrifices and oblations listed in the Leviticus, a rite not explicitly mentioned in the canonical Scriptures but abundantly described in later Jewish literature was probably made an integral part of the temple

---

[18] An eighth day was added to the original seven of the feast.
[19] *The Siddur,* edited by R. David de Sola Pool (New York, 1960).

ceremonial for the feast of tabernacles: the priests would lead a solemn procession down to Siloam and draw water for the libations on the altar of burnt-offerings. About this ritual, the Talmud grows lyrical: "He who has not seen the rejoicing at the fountain has not witnessed joy in his life. At the close of the first day of tabernacles, priests and Levites descended to the court of the women.... Men rich in piety and good deeds danced before them with lighted torches in their hands, singing songs of praise. And levites without number with harps, lyres, cymbals, trumpets and other musical instruments, stood on the steps leading down from the court of Israel to the court of the women, fifteen in number, as the fifteen gradual psalms" (treatise *Sukkah* 51 b).

We have remarked earlier that the short interval between passover and the feast of weeks made it difficult for the householders from distant regions of Palestine to leave their homes twice in seven weeks, and this in the midst of the harvest. The feast of tabernacles would put them to less inconvenience, as the labor in olive groves and vineyards was virtually over. The autumn festival would be eagerly awaited and attended, perhaps to the detriment of the feast of weeks, by all who were in a condition to "ascend to Jerusalem" for the tabernacles, while their less fortunate fellow villagers would celebrate at home under their *sukkoth*. A certain decline in the popularity of the feast of weeks has been observed by Jewish scholars, and a corresponding increase in the popularity of tabernacles, especially under the aspect of a Sinaitic memorial. This is further substantiated by the fact that the *Tishrî* festivals duplicated and, so to speak "captured" a number of features which originally belonged to the feast of weeks; thus the sprays of foliage on the pavement of the synagogues, the waving of palms and branches; note also the similarity between the hymns of the synagogue for the feast of weeks and for the *Simbath Tôrah*. Traces of this evolution may be detected in the Fourth Gospel, inasmuch as St. John relates the deeds and discourses of Christ in a chronological framework of which the temple festivals mark the rhythm, and this in turn may have influenced the choice of Gospel readings in our Orthodox liturgy.[20]

HANUKKAH. In addition to the festivals prescribed by the Tôrah, the Jews of the Hellenistic period observed the anniversary of the purification of the temple of Zerubbabel following its desecration by Antiochus Épiphanes. Unlike the regular pilgrimages of the Law, it has no connnection with the agricultural cycle but is essentially a historical memorial. In 145 of the Seleucid era (= 167 B.C.), Antiochus and the Syrians invaded the temple and erected an altar on which sacrifices were offered to Zeus Olympios, a Hellenized Syro-Phenician Ba'al Shamaïm (1 Macc 1:54; 2 Macc 6:2-6). Three years later,[21] in 148 of the Seleucid era (= 164 B.C.), the Jewish patriots having defeated the Syrians, the temple was purified, a new altar was built for the burnt-offerings, and Judas Maccabee and the elders decreed that the purification of the temple should be commemorated annually (1 Macc 4:42-59; 2 Macc 10:5-8; Josephus Antiquities 12, 7:7, n° 323-326). The new feast, the *hanukkah*, τὰ ἐγκαίνια, became extremely popular, yet did not rate a festal *ordo* for the service of the altar in addition to the daily sacrifices, since it was not a Tôrah festival. It lasted eight full days, beginning on the anniversary date, the twenty-fifth of *Kislew* (December). The celebration duplicated several rites and customs of the feast of tabernacles, so that it is surnamed in 2 Maccabees 1:9 the "tabernacles of *Kislew*". Festive throngs of worshippers carrying torches and waving palms marched in procession through the courts of the temple, singing hymns and the Great Hallel: "Holding green boughs, tighten ye your rounds up to the horns of the altar" (Ps 118:27). A distinctive feature of the *hanukkah* was the lighting of lamps, one for each day of the week, hence its popular name of "feast of lights". The older clay lamps are replaced in modern Jewish homes by nine-branched candlesticks of silver, of a design similar to

---

[20] See my article "Scriptural Readings for Mid-Pentecost and Pentecost", *St. Vladimir's Theological Quarterly* 21/3 (1977), pp. 148-159.

[21] Or "two years", according to a divergent reading, possibly a copyist's error, in 2 Maccabees 10:3.

the heraldic *menôrah* of the temple and the synagogues. The lighting of the fire on the new altar and of the *hanukkah* lamps were the object of stories having their roots in post-exilic legends: one recalled how a party of explorers sent by Nehemiah had discovered in a secret cave an oily liquid which, when hit by the rays of the sun, miraculously blazed and set afire the wood on the altar of Zerubbabel (2 Macc 1:18-23). A Talmudic source (*Pesiktâ Rabbah* 2) quotes a similar miracle on the eve of the consecration of the new altar: a small vessel of oil, sealed and hidden away from the Syrians, was found by the Hasmonaean priests, who used it to relight the *menôrah*.

Theories on the possible adaptation of the Jewish *hanukkah* to a pagan feast of the winter solstice are extremely questionable. The Roman celebration of the *Sol Invictus* on December 25 may, to a certain measure, explain the dating of Christmas in western Christianity; but the arguments advanced to set the Jewish feast in direct relation with a solstice rite are too far-fetched and too fragile to be of much value for an understanding of the *hanukkah* festival, whose foundation in history is unusually firm and leaves little or nothing to be desired.[22]

The festal calendar of the Jews, which we have outlined in this chapter, forms the framework of Jesus' labors as recorded by the four evangelists. It remains for us, in the succeeding chapters, to join the company of the disciples as they went up to Jerusalem and to follow the one who, in his human and his divine nature, was both the pilgrim and the Lord of the temple.

---

[22] See the discussion in R. de Vaux, *Ancient Israel* II, p. 513. It might be just as well to let these theories disappear in the limbo of unprofitable speculations.

CHAPTER FIVE

"They Went Up To Jerusalem"

A "LIFE OF JESUS" ought to pay very special attention to
pages of the Gospel in which the evangelists have recorded
the "ascents" of the Lord to Jerusalem and the instances in
which he appeared in the temple; perhaps more than any
other passages of the New Testament, they reveal in a human
context the mystery of his person and of his mission, setting
in a unique light the enocunter of the Old Testament institutions with the new order which he came to usher in. But is
it at all possible to write a historical biography of Jesus? It
has been attempted by many, and some "lives" are regarded
as literary masterpieces. There is indeed enough material in
the New Testament writings for drawing a vivid portrait of
Jesus. However, the tradition of the earliest Christian groups,
preached by the apostles and recorded by the evangelists, is
insufficient for a "life of Jesus", if we mean by this a detailed
historical biography. Only Matthew and Luke relate the circumstances of the birth of Jesus and some episodes of his early
childhood. This explains in part the popular craving to
learn more about it all, and accounts for the gullibility of
foreign visitors ready to accept uncritically the fabrications
of an apocryphal literature often inspired by questionable
ideologies and circulated by the professional guides of the
Jerusalem pilgrimage. We know nothing of the thirty years or
so passed in the obscurity of Nazareth, save that Jesus was
working as a carpenter, and that he was not known to have
received any other instruction but that of the common folks
who frequented the synagogue.

The words and deeds of Jesus during the short years of
his so-called public life are recorded in loosely connected episodes, selected and edited by the evangelists, each according to

his own plan, method of composition, and the formal aspect of Jesus' life which he wished to emphasize. Hence discrepancies between the four Gospels, which ought neither to be laboriously harmonized,[1] nor to be regarded as making doubtful the overall validity of the record. As St. Augustine puts it, "Is it essential that one author should relate the same events in the very order in which they occurred or in a different order, as long as he does not contradict himself or his fellow writers? . . . It is probable that each of the evangelists believed he was writing what God gave him to remember, the substance rather than this or that particular order, and this impairs in no way the authority of the Gospel." [2]

The order in which the evangelists have recorded the words and deeds of Jesus is, by the very nature of the object, a broad chronological order, following the human development of the Master, from childhood, adolescence and adulthood to his passion, death and resurrection, but this chronological framework is all but rigorous. Indeed, St. Luke was concerned with setting the fact of Jesus' life in relation to historical, even cosmic events. Thus he traced the ancestry of Christ not only to "Abraham son of Terah" but to "Adam son of God" (3:23-38). He dated the nativity in reference to a census taken by Quirinius (Κυρηνιός), governor of the Roman province of Syria (Luke 2:1-2) — a fact in principle verifiable, but whose precision escapes us due to the incompleteness of our historical information.[3] Luke's multiple syn-

---

[1] "Synopses" of the four Gospels, on the other hand, do not aim at an artificial harmonization of the different traditions, but at making easier a comparison of the texts.

[2] *De consensu evangelistarum.* P.L. 34, col. 1102.

[3] Quirinius (Κυρηνιός) identified as Publius Sulpicius Quirinius, may have been governor of Syria, *legatus Augusti pro-praetore*, as early as 3-2 B.C., and he may have undertaken the "first census" of Luke 2:1-2 at that early stage of his career, the detail of which remains most uncertain. According to Josephus (Antiquities XVII 13:6, n° 355), he was sent by Augustus to take a census of the province for the purpose of taxation, and to evaluate (and confiscate) the revenues of the tetrarchy of Archelaus, who had been deposed by the emperor in A.D. 6. This census of A.D. 6-7 cannot be the one used by Luke for fixing the date of the Nativity, since it is certain that Jesus was born before the death of Herod the Great, which occurred in 4 B.C. (= 750 of the foundation of Rome). One should remember that our Christian era as calculated by the sixth-century monk Dionysius Exiguus is some four years late in

chronisms in the opening verses of chapter 3 mean to give us an approximate date for the baptism in the Jordan and constitute a solemn introduction to Jesus' public life: He was by then "about thirty years old", ὡσεὶ ἐτῶν τριάκοντα (Luke 3:23). Most of the time the Gospels, in relating the various episodes of Jesus' life, use connecting formulae as vague as "in these days", "after this", and the like. Exceptionally, St. John somehow dates the journeys of Jesus and his disciples to Jerusalem by stating that it was passover-time, or the tabernacles, or the *hanukkah*, but these otherwise valuable notations are of little help toward solving the problem of the duration of Jesus ministry, whether over one year, or over two years, or over three. And it is a fact that the evangelists took liberties with a chronological order, for which they substituted often a topical one, each of them according to his special purpose or mode of presentation.[4] Let us face it: their interest was not with time-tables, but with the substance and meaning of the Gospel.

Vivid character studies of heroes and saints have been written with a documentation often as lacunous as the Gospel narratives; a familiarity with the historical background enabled their authors to evoke the atmosphere, nay the aura surrounding the great figures of the past. I have in mind, as an example among many, Joergensen's Life of St. Francis, based on the legend of the three companions, the testimony of Bonaventura and the *Fioretti*, with the benefit of modern research in the history and sociology of the Middle Ages. Could something similar be done about Jesus Christ on the basis of a

comparison with the real date. As for the dating of the baptism in the Jordan, the fifteenth year of Tiberius (A.D. 28-29), Jesus being about thirty years of age, ὡσεὶ ἐτῶν τριάκοντα, this is another approximation by St. Luke; actually Jesus must have been somewhat older, as we would say: "in his early thirties".

[4] St. Mark cared little about setting his narratives in a chronological framework or in a systematic order. St. Matthew, while composing his Gospel in the general order of events, tried to group the various episodes into topical categories: miracles, the parables of the lake, the exhortations to vigilance during the week of the Passion. St. Luke preferred a geographical order: the Gospel being proclaimed from Galilee to Jerusalem, and from Jerusalem to "the ends of the earth". St. John was attentive to the annual rhythm of the great feasts of the Jews.

thorough exegesis of the Gospel and modern biblical scholar-
ship? Would the figure of Jesus become more intelligible to
us, eager as we are to penetrate the secret of what is usually
called his "personality"? I write this word within quotation
marks; we usually understand by it the sum of a person's
peculiarities, of whatever origin they may be: genes, environ-
ment, education; any distinctive trait which develops in a man
and gives him a profile that is his own. Reduced to these
features, a picture of Christ still would not be a finished portrait, but only a raw charcoal outline thrown on the canvas
by an uncertain hand; it would reveal the personality of the
artist much more than that of Jesus himself. Similarly a writer's arrangement of selected episodes would be his own rather
than the evangelists', whose objective was not to write a biography but to proclaim the Good News, under the inspiration
of the Holy Spirit and from the unique vantage point of the
resurrection. A biography, whether mystical or apologetical,
eulogistic or critical, would always be inadequate and could
not possibly avoid a measure of artificiality and arbitrariness.
This is because of the very transcendence of the person of
Christ.

Each page of the Gospel shows us Jesus Christ acting
through the instrumentality of his human nature, soul and
body, but his activities are ascribed to his divine person as
their first and ultimate subject, which belongs not in the realm
of creatures; his acts are the acts of God. The eternally-begot-
ten of the Father became man, that he might heal our wounds
and make us fulfill our destiny as "children of the Most High"
(Ps 82:6) ; he became one of us without forfeiting his divinity,
yet veiling it by the condescension of a divine economy, lest
we be dazzled by his unbearable radiance. His personality is
from beyond history and remains inscrutable, but the historian
is not at liberty to ignore or by-pass the testimony of the New
Testament and the tradition of the Church, defended by the
Fathers and defined by the ecumenical councils; this testimony
and this tradition, formally considered, are in themselves
historical facts regardless of their object, which is indeed an
object of faith, not to be apprehended by the discipline of
history, but neither to be rejected a priori.

The mystery of the duality of natures in Christ the God-man, and of the unity of the divine person, revealed in the Gospel and perceived from the beginning by the Christians, was expressed with increasing precision by the Church Fathers. The progress of doctrine, however, is not to be understood as a quantitative growth of the revealed datum, as if each generation of Christians added something of its own, but as a reflex of defense against misinterpretations which would constitute a betrayal of the Gospel.

It is neither within the scope of this book nor within the competence of this writer to review the development of Christological doctrine, but we wish to state here this our conviction: that the dogma of the incarnation, in its essence and in its consequences for the salvation of mankind, as it came to be formulated by the Fathers and as it is professed by the one, holy, catholic and apostolic Church, is the very substance of the Evangel, to be discovered through the inspired accounts of Jesus' birth and infancy, and the dramatic episodes of his public life.

Our excuse for this lengthy preamble is our desire to usher our fellow Christians into the heart of the Gospel message, lest perhaps they read "the story" and remain mere spectators of the drama, personally uninvolved. The Gospel must be for all of us something more than the illustrated edition of a "life of Jesus".

THE MEETING OF OUR LORD IN THE TEMPLE ('Υπαπαντή) "When the time came for *their* purification according to the law of Moses, *they* brought *him* up to Jerusalem to present *him* to the Lord" (Lk 2:22 RSV). At first sight, and supposing the pronouns "their", "they", "him" duly identified without the benefit of the Greek case-endings, the story is deceptively simple, but we are soon going to discover that its interpretation raises serious problems. To begin with, a textual one: the bulk of the Greek manuscripts, followed by our English versions, reads: "the days of *their* purification", namely of Mary and her new-born son, αἱ ἡμέραι τοῦ καθαρισμοῦ αὐτῶν, yet a few "western" manuscripts have the singlar αὐτοῦ, "of *his* [Jesus'] purification", a read-

ing adopted by the Latin Vulgate, *dies purgationis eius.* But
the presentation of Jesus to the temple can hardly be called a
"purification". In reality, the story as told by St. Luke, no
matter which reading we adopt, combines two distinct yet
related rituals: the purification of a woman from the legal
impurity contracted by her giving birth to a child, and the
redeeming of a first-born son to the price of five shekels, as a
sign of his consecration to Yahweh (Lev 12:2-8; Ex 13:11-13;
Num 18:15-16). Both rituals would normally be performed
at the consecrated place of worship, that is, for the period
following the effective centralization of the cult, the temple
of Jerusalem. We hinted earlier at the probability of special
provisions for Israelites from the diaspora or from distant
provinces (see ch. 4). But the vicinity of Bethlehem where,
as St. Luke supposes, the holy family remained for some time
after the birth of Jesus, would have made it possible for them
to abide by the letter of the Law.

We see no way of reconciling St. Luke's sequence of events
with that of Matthew. Luke says nothing of the visit of the
Magi, Herod's persecution, and the flight into Egypt. Matthew
makes no mention of the circumcision on the eighth day and
of the presentation in the temple. If we insist on fusing the
two stories into a single narrative, we might place the presentation to the temple at some undetermined time before
the adoration of the Magi, the slaying of the children of
Bethlehem and the flight of the holy family, which must have
followed in rapid succession. This plausible harmonization of
Matthew and Luke had already been attempted by St. Augustine. But in fact neither of the two evangelists intended
to write a day-by-day account, such as would provide the material for a historical biography or establish the facts for
an official life-record. St. Matthew's aim was to show in the
episodes of the Gospel the realization of messianic prophecies from the Old Testament: "This was to fulfill what
the Lord had spoken by the prophet," "Thus was fulfilled
which had been spoken by the prophet," or similar formulae.
St. Luke preferred to look ahead to the spread of the Gospel
and the future realization of long-range prophecies. Different
as they are, the accounts of the birth and childhood of Christ

according to Matthew and Luke offer a valid authentication of the divinity and mission of Jesus, the common intent of the evangelists being to show the Church on the march toward the consummation of the kingdom foretold by the Law and the prophets.

The feast commemorating the presentation of Jesus in the temple is called in the West "Feast of the Purification of the Blessed Virgin Mary"; in Eastern Orthodoxy, "Feast of the Meeting of Our Lord Jesus Christ in the Temple". The former title stresses the compliance of the holy family with the precepts of the Law; the latter, the coming forward of the elder Simeon and Ann the prophetess to meet the holy family at the entrance of the sanctuary, the Ὑπαπαντή. These shades of semantics affect in no way the essence of the celebration which in either liturgy expresses the Christological dogma in its integrity, as the Christ-child, on the arms of his mother, makes his first entrance into the temple.

The action is at the entrance of what Josephus calls the "inner *hiéron*", that is, the courtyards surrounding the "house of Yahweh", in contradistinction to the common area accessible to all, Jews and non-Jews alike. We should not imagine a building resembling the portal of a Gothic cathedral, with a high priest in full regalia receiving the holy family, as in medieval stained glass windows or Renaissance paintings.[5] The offerings presented by the Leviticus 12:6 were "a yearling lamb, for the holocaust, and a young pigeon or a turtle dove as a sin offering". Those who could not afford the price of a lamb would bring a pair of doves in satisfaction of the Law (Lew 12:8). This is the offering that Joseph and Mary, having paid their five shekels for the redemption of the firstborn, presented to the priest on duty at the gate of the women's court, from where they saw the altar in front of the "house" (see above, ch. 3).

Dramatis personae: Simeon and Anna. Simeon, a righteous and devout old man. The Holy Spirit, inspirer of prophets, was upon him. He looked for the "consolation of

[5] The archaeological accuracy of the icons of the "Meeting" is totally immaterial, for the art of the icon is essentially spiritual, and its effectiveness does not depend on realistic representations.

Israel", παράκλησιν; this word is reminiscent of Isaiah 40:1, "Console ye, console ye my people!" The New English Bible (1961) translates the words of Luke by "the *restoration* of Israel". This is in fact what the majority of the Jews in the time of Jesus understood, and this is how the Babylonian exiles had interpreted Isaiah; but the prophets, and now Simeon, were looking for a spiritual revival with or beyond the final resurrection.[6] The latter meaning is most certainly the one intended by the evangelist reporting Simeon's expectation. Thus is the Christian messianic faith, having its roots in the prophets, sharply set apart from the Jewish dream of an earthly ruler over a temporal kingdom.

Late Judaism had little use for prophets; the Tôrah was deemed sufficient for the instruction of the people. "Since Haggai, Zechariah, and Malachi died, the Holy Spirit has ceased in Israel" (Talmud, *Sôtah* 45 b), and private revelations were of no value for juridical determinations. On the contrary, the entire episode of the "meeting" is presented by Luke as a continuous chain of authentic prophecies.

Nothing in the Gospel narrative indicates that Simeon came to the temple in an official capacity, as some mediaeval exegetes and iconographers have imagined. Several *stichera* in our liturgical books call him "the elder" ὁ πρέσβυς, πρεσβύτης, but these titles do not imply that he was invested with sacral dignity, as medieval authors and western iconographers have suggested; the expression ἱερεὺς πρεσ-βύτης καὶ δίκαιος, which Mother Mary translates in *The Festal Menaion* (1969) by "the priest and righteous elder", is rather a late amplification of the primitive tradition. St. Luke regards Simeon as a simple man revered for his age, his character and his devotion. Nor is the meeting in the temple an effect of chance. Simeon, who had received from the Holy Spirit the assurance that he would not die before seeing "the Christ of the Lord", is brought into the temple by the same Holy Spirit, even as Mary and Joseph enter the sacred courts. Taking the child up in his arms, he proclaims his faith, his

[6] G. Barrois, *The Face of Christ in the Old Testament* (St. Vladimir's Seminary Press, 1974), pp. 119-120.

hope and his secret expectation in the prophetic canticle commonly known as the *Nunc Dimittis* (Luke 2:29-32).

> Lord, now lettest thou thy servant depart in peace
> according to thy word!
> For mine eyes have seen thy salvation
> which thou hast prepared before the face of all people,
> a light to lighten the Gentiles
> and the glory of thy people Israel.

We read or chant the canticle of Simeon at Vespers, and the Roman Breviary prescribes it for Compline, the monastic evening prayer. The theme of light is particularly emphasized, both in the Eastern and Western liturgies. Thus the prophet Isaiah is made to exclaim, in the fifth canticle of the festal canon: "I have seen beforehand God made flesh, Lord of the light that knows no evening and king of peace" (transl. by Mother Mary). In the West, at the solemn Mass of the feast, the wax candles offered by the faithful for the service of the altar are blessed by the celebrant, hence the popular name of "Candlemas" given to the feast or, in French-speaking countries, *la Chandeleur*.

The canticle sounds a note of universality: salvation has been prepared "before the face" or "in the sight of all people". This extension of the covenant to all mankind had been foretold by the post-exilic prophets, especially by the continuator of Isaiah, for whom Israel was not the exclusive beneficiary, but rather the privileged instrument of common salvation. "Salvation is from the Jews," Jesus would say to the Samaritan woman at the well of Jacob (John 4:22), for the Jews were the keepers of the revelation to Moses, and "from their people Christ was born according to the flesh" (Rom 9:5).

An oracle recorded in Isaiah 41:4 had already given us a key to the economy of the prophetic revelation. Prophecies do not stand isolated, they come in clusters. Promises made of old by God warrant the reality of future events foretold by the prophets, lest they be regarded as mere chance events or utopian dreams without substance. Only God can forge the unbreakable link between the past and that which will come to pass, "for I, Yahweh, the First; I with the latter ages, I am He" (Is 41:4). And it is the same key which opens unto us the mystery of the incarnation: the child in the arms of Simeon is he whom the prophets have announced, of whose birth the elder was given a premonition, and who would be the Savior of mankind. The consummation of the mystery lies beyond human history; it is the "life of the world to come".

But one more testimony had to be borne by Simeon: "This child is set for the fall and rising of many in Israel," an object of contradiction among the Jews, whose passionate taking of sides will become particularly dramatic during the short years of his public life, in confrontation with the Pharisees and the authorities of the temple. In little more than three decades, he will be led to the rock of Calvary; Mary will stand near the cross and share in his agony: "A sword shall pierce through her soul also." The prophetic words of Simeon forewarn the young mother, lest she be assailed by doubt or despair in the hour of the ultimate dereliction of her son, who will cry with a loud voice, "My God, my God, why hast thou forsaken me?" (Matthew 27:46).

The Western Church commemorates the "Compassion of the Blessed Virgin Mary" on the Friday before Holy Week, and her "Seven Sorrows" (*Festum septem dolorum B.M.V.*) on the fifteenth of September — the morrow of the Exaltation of the Holy Cross. Both celebrations are very popular in Hispanic countries, where the baptismal name *Dolores* is frequently given to girls.

"And there was a prophetess, Anna" (Lk 2:36). There had always been women whom the Spirit of God had inspired to exhort and to lead the people in critical times. Miriam the sister of Aaron had taken her timbrel to celebrate the miraculous escape from bondage at the crossing of the Red Sea (Ex 15:20-21). Deborah had been a judge in Israel and sang her hymn of victory when the united tribes defeated the Canaanites at the river Kishon (Judges 4:4 and ch. 5). Huldah the prophetess, answering to a request of Josiah's courtiers, sanctioned in the name of Yahweh the religious reformation undertaken by the king, following the fortuitous discovery of the book of the Tôrah in the temple (2 Kings 22:14-20). Another

Hannah, the mother of Samuel, had intoned a hymn of magnification to the Providence of God "who raises the poor from the dust", "who will give strength to the king and exalt the power of his anointed" (1 Sam 2:1-10).

"There was a prophetess, Anna, the daughter of Phanuel, of the tribe of 'Asher"; she was of advanced age, a widow after seven years of marriage, now eighty-four years old; an ascetic, fasting and praying night and day in the temple, from which she never departed (Luke 2:36-37). This detail given by the evangelist should probably not be taken literally, as if Anna had arranged for herself a little cubby hole in some remote corner of the sanctuary, as some exegetes have imagined.[7] The devout men and women whom one sees day after day at any odd hour in the church of the Holy Sepulcher would be a valid analogy, if one excludes some eccentrics, a nuisance to the Greek and Latin sextons of the basilica.

"And coming up that very hour she gave thanks to God, and spoke of him [the child] to all who were looking for the redemption of Jerusalem" (Luke 2:38). The meaning is clear: for Luke, Anna is moved, as was Simeon, by a secret instinct; no blind chance, no collusion or premeditation either. Like Simeon, she had always hoped for the redemption of Israel, λύτρωσις, that is "deliverance through ransom"; and behold, he who is that ransom, of whom she speaks freely to everyone, is here, on the arms of the old man. Sophisticated interpretations of the text — too many have been attempted by radical exegetes — do unwarranted violence to the general meaning of the episode narrated by Luke, and need not be considered here. Through St. Luke's craftsmanship as a historian, the Gospel message is secured: two witnesses of the age-old expectation of the people, endowed with the charism of the prophets, proclaim that the time has come; and the evangelist records the earliest tradition of the Church with the authority of scriptural inspiration.

"THEY FOUND HIM IN THE TEMPLE". When Jesus was twelve years old, they took him to the annual pilgrimage

[7] M. J. Lagrange, *L'Evangile selon Saint Luc* (1921), p. 91.

for passover (Lk 2:41-50).[8] It would be a long journey, in
the company of other people from Nazareth, some seventy
miles, on foot or riding donkeys. The direct road crosses the
plain of Jezreel and winds along the crest of the Palestinian
highlands through Samaria, the Mountain of Ephraïm, and
Benjamin; they would stop at roadside inns or camp out for
the night. St. Luke does not describe the journey, nor the
detail of the festivities in Jerusalem. These were familiar
enough to Jewish readers and had otherwise little or no bearing on the story. When the feast was ended, they set out to
return home, but the child Jesus tarried in Jerusalem. Supposing he was with some of their company, they went one day's
journey and looked for him among their relatives. Not finding
him, they turned back to Jerusalem and after three days found
him in the temple, sitting in a group of teachers, "listening
to them and asking them questions", as was fitting on the part
of a twelve-year-old lad. "The bystanders were amazed at his
intelligence and his responses," ἀποκρίσεις; the Greek term
should not make us imagine anything like a rabbinical debate,
but rather a sympathetic exchange of questions and answers
between old masters and an unusually bright youngster. The
story as told by Luke is insufficient to support the weight of
theologizing on the problem of the "science of Christ". It
continues on the same low key: Mary's mild reproach, "How
could you do this to us?" and Jesus' pert retort, "Do you not
know that I must be about my Father's business?" (Lk 2:49
KJ) or, in the rendering of RSV, "Did you not know that I
must be in my Father's house?" [9] We read here in Jesus' own
words the first affirmation, indirect but absolute, of his divine
filiation.

"But they did not understand what he was saying to them."
His mother, adds St. Luke, "kept all these things in her heart,
pondering them" (Lk 2:19, 51); there was here a mystery
she could not grasp, nor any human. The day when Jesus was

---

[8] In late Judaism the age of accountability for boys before the Law was
fixed at thirteen years completed, when the young Israelite was declared *bâr-
mitsvah*.

[9] The latter interpretation is suggested by the context, rather than being
a straight translation of the Greek.

found in the temple after three days of a frantic search was not for her without shadow, for the ominous prophecy of Simeon had engraved itself deep in her consciousness. Only the resurrection and the miracle of Pentecost would dissipate her fears and her apprehension, and bring unto her and unto all believers the peace which the world cannot know.

Luke's record of the "meeting in the temple" and of Jesus being found in the midst of the rabbis points unambiguously to the double aspect of the dogma of the incarnation. Christ "emptied himself", ἑαυτὸν ἐκένωσεν, of the attributes of his divine nature, and we are made aware of his divinity through the sole testimony of those who witnessed his miracles, the prophecies concerning him or, on rare occasions, his direct answers to those who challenged him. He assumed all our limitations and infirmities, sharing in our temptations, "taking up the form of a slave" (Phil 2:7). We see him as a babe submitted to the obligations of the Law; redeemed, he who is the Redeemer; a passover pilgrim in Jerusalem, entering not as a sinner to be reconciled, but as the Lord of the house; the Latin liturgy for the feast proclaims it: "Behold, he comes into his holy temple, the Lord of Lords." [10]

---

[10] *Ecce venit ad templum sanctum suum dominator dominus*, from the Roman breviary, matins of the feast of the Purification.

CHAPTER SIX

Pilgrim and Lord of the Temple

ST. JOHN'S CHRONOLOGY. The authors of the Gospels did not organize the recording of Jesus' words and deeds in strict chronological sequence. The scanty synchronisms or time notations in the Gospel according to St. Luke or in the Fourth Gospel do not amount to a chronological system such as our contemporaries would require for a "life of Jesus". St. Mark did nor care about a systematic ordering; he simply wrote down what he had heard from Peter, together with miscellaneous sayings of the Lord transmitted by oral tradition and possibly gathered by St. Matthew in a collection of so-called *Logia*, originally in Aramaic language. The Greek Gospel according to St. Matthew shows forth a topical organization: traditions on Jesus' birth, several series of parables, the Sermon on the Mount, and miracles. St. Luke's interest was to trace the genesis of Christian revelation from Nazareth to Jerusalem, which would become the starting point of the preaching of the Gospel to all peoples, and the cradle of the Church universal. A few synchronisms in Luke's Gospel and in the Book of Acts aim at setting the development of Christianity in relation to the course of world history, but we are left in the dark concerning the duration and dates of Jesus' public life.[1]

The Fourth Gospel represents a further step in the Christian proclamation of the "Good News", *kerygma*, which had by then become a full-fledged catechesis. St. John, or the editor of the Johannine "corpus" — Orthodox tradition identifies

---

[1] For a summary of the so-called "synoptic problem" and a critical appraisal of the Fourth Gospel, see V. Kesich, *The Gospel Image of Christ* (St. Vladimir's Seminary Press, 1972), pp. 41-44, and the sections of introduction to the Synoptics and the Fourth Gospel in the *Bible of Jerusalem*.

him with Prochorus (Acts 6:5) — times the episodes of the Fourth Gospel in reference to the festivals and pilgrimages of the Jews, which we have listed in chapter 4. If we make some allowance for unimportant variations, redactional transpositions or insertion of minor episodes, a uniform pattern can easily be detected: a notable deed or miracle becomes the occasion for an extensive discourse in rhythmic prose, developing systematically a doctrinal theme. At each step of his narrative, the evangelist notes how the suspicion and hostility of the Jewish leaders and of the crowd [2] grows to a climax of hatred as the drama nears its end; this may explain why the literary scheme clearly apparent in the early chapters of the Gospel becomes blurred in the latter chapters, as the discourses of the Master are violently interrupted by his adversaries. Incomplete and uncertain as they are, the time-notations which tie up the account of the miracles and the teaching of Christ with the course of the festal year, especially when he ascended to Jerusalem for the temple celebrations, may help us to devise an ever so tentative chronology of the Fourth Gospel.

We may list as follows the literary units of the Fourth Gospel prefaced by a time-notation.

1. A passover "at hand" (John 2:13). Jesus drives the vendors and money changers out of the temple (2:13-22). Nicodemus, a Sanhedrite, visits Jesus by night; discourse on the birth unto the "life in the Spirit" (3:1-21).

2. "... a feast of the Jews", ἑορτή τῶν Ἰουδαίων or with the definite article, ἡ ἑορτή, "*the* feast of the Jews" (5:1). Is that feast *par excellence* another passover, or the feast of tabernacles, *sukkoth*, often referred to in the Old Testament as "*the* feast", *hé-hâg* without further qualification? Or is the anonymous feast of the received text the "feast of weeks", *shabû'oth*, i.e. pentecost, according to an hypothesis advanced by Fr. Lagrange and the Jerusalem Bible? Jesus heals a paralytic at the pool of Bethzata (5:5-9). He

---

[2] Jewish leaders, namely the priests and lawyers hostile to Jesus, and the mob, are referred to in the Fourth Gospel as "the Jews". No deliberate anti-semitism here. St. John never denied that Jesus counted enthusiastic partisans among the crowd, and some, more reserved, in temple circles.

answers to the Jews angered "not only because he had broken
the sabbath, but also called God his own father" (verse 18);
discourse on the works of the Son, which bear witness to his
divine origin and mission (5:19-47).

3. "Passover . . . at hand'", in Galilee (6:4). Jesus feeds
five thousand persons on five barley loaves and two fishes
(6:1-14); discourse on the bread of life, in the synagogue of
Capernaum (6:31-40). Jesus' response to the Jews murmuring:
"How can this man give us his flesh to eat?" Divided reactions of the bystanders (6:41-46).

4. "The Jews' feast of tabernacles was at hand" (7:2);
"toward the middle of the feast" (7:14); "on the last day
of the feast" (7:37). This section does not conform exactly
with the format of the preceding three. St. John notes a gross
incomprehension among the followers of Jesus, division among
the people, and open hostility on the part of the Jewish leaders. No miracle is reported; fragments of discourses are given
as Jesus taught in the temple, much to the astonishment of
the Jews and the anger of the rabbis, who fear his influence
on the masses and challenge the authority of his doctrine.

5. The following section is built on the regular pattern
of units 1-3. A miracle: the healing of a man born blind
(9:1-38); after a brief interval, the discourse, which this time
is an extended parable: Jesus the good shepherd (10:1-18).
By some freak of redaction or transmission of the text, the
time-notation was omitted. The miracle had taken place at
the pool of Siloam, where the waters of Gihôn were channel-
led through the underground aqueduct of king Ezechias. We
may recall how the Mishnah describes the solemn procession
of priests and levites coming down to draw water for the
ceremonial washing of the altar and the libations during the
octave of tabernacles (see above, ch. 4). The feast of tabernacles had always been extremely popular; in the parlance of
American Judaism, the celebrations which follow one another
during the month of *Tishrî* (September-October) are the "high
holy days". We find here a possible clue for supplying the
missing time-notation of unit 5. Would not the blind man
have been healed during the festivities of tabernacles? Meanwhile the stormy discussion continues. To those who question

or deny the authority of his teaching, Jesus affiirms his unique
filiation, the authenticity of his mission and the truth of his
message.

6. This again would be the theme of his teaching in the
temple, under the portico of Solomon, during the feast of the
dedication, *hanukkah*, in winter (10:22-28). Since the last
autumn, the hostility of the mob had increased in violence.
Twice they had picked up stones to hurl at him, and he had
escaped by leaving the temple area and Jerusalem for a time.
The leaders, bent upon getting rid of him, bided their time
and considered haw this could best be achieved, if possible
in a manner which would keep the appearance of legality and
not alarm prematurely the Roman overlords. We shall review
in the next chapter the events of Jesus' last week on earth,
from the messianic entry into the city to the cross and the
resurrection on the third day.

The above listing of "timed" units does not constitute,
strictly speaking, a chronology of the Fourth Gospel. We still
do not know for sure the duration of Jesus' public life. The
Fourth Gospel mentions three passovers, perhaps four if,
instead of the un-named feast in John 5:1, we accept the var-
iant "*the* feast", and interpret it as one more passover. If we
choose this reading, though it be ill-supported by the manuscript tradition,[3] Jesus' ministry, from his baptism in the
Jordan to his death on the cross, would have lasted three full
years and a fraction, since the ascent to Jerusalem reported in
John 2:13 was obviously not the first act of Jesus public life,
which began, according to the Synoptics, immediately after
the baptism. It is unlikely that it took that long for his enemies
to make up their minds; the rapid escalation of hatred against
Jesus, noted by all the evangelists, is particularly evident in
the Fourth Gospel.

Counting with the three passovers of the Fourth Gospel,
we would obtain for the duration of Jesus' public activity a
total of two full years and a fraction, which seems the most
likely option. It is true that the Synoptics know only one pas-

---

[3] The reading "the feast", ἡ ἑορτή (John 5:1), is rejected by the
majority of critics. There is little evidence for identifying the anonymous feast
with the passover or the feast of tabernacles.

sover, viz. the one of passion week. But an attempt at reconciling the Synoptics and the Fourth Gospel seems futile and is
probably inadvisable. At any rate, reducing the public life of
Christ to one year would force us to cram within too short
a period all the episodes recorded by the four evangelists and
a considerable time spent at travelling to and fro in Palestine,
through Galilee, the district of Jordan, and up to Jerusalem.[4]
It certainly would not do justice to St. John's formal intention
of "timing" the Master's notable deeds, miracles and discourses. As a matter of fact, St. John's time-notations, as well
as the precise identification of places, apparently with little
or no doctrinal consequence and jotted down for no other
reason than "that is the way it happened", are a recognized
characteristic of his Gospel.

On the basis of what precedes, we might outline the chronology of Jesus' public life as follows, using the tables and
comments of the Jerusalem Bible.

Baptism of Jesus and return to Galilee, autumn 27.

Passover 28 (John 2:13).

"A feast", feast of weeks, or tabernacles, 28 (John 5:1).

Passover 29, in Galilee (John 6:4).

Tabernacles, autumn 29 (John 7:2).

Feast of the dedication (*hanukkah*), December 29 (John
10:22).

Passover, 30 (John 11:55).

We give these dates with all due reservation, merely for the
sake of illustration. They remain hypothetical and add very
little to St. John's scheme, which we intend to use as a framework for the next paragraphs of this chapter.

MERCHANTS IN THE TEMPLE. The Synoptics place
the expulsion of the merchants from the temple immediately
after the triumphal entry of Jesus into the city, on the first day
of passion week. According to the Fourth Gospel (2:13-17),
it occurred at the very beginning of his public life, following
the baptism in the Jordan and the return to Galilee, from
whence Jesus would go up to Jerusalem for the first passover

[4] *The Interpreter's Bible*, vol. I, pp. 151-152. *The Interpreter's Dictionary
of the Bible*, vol. I, pp. 601-602.

recorded in John 2:13. It is of course the same episode, reported together with the same Old Testament quotations and
Jesus' prophecy of the destruction of the temple, whose monumental stones had impressed the disciples. The order of the
Synoptics intends to be chronological, as they place the story
of the merchants driven out of the temple shortly before the
passion. But St. John, by placing the episode at the beginning
of Jesus' public life, is theologically motivated. As Professor
Kesich writes in his book *The Gospel Image of Christ* (St.
Vladimir's Press, 1972, p. 56) "he may have chosen the cleans-
ing of the temple as a major symbolic act, indicating that
the life of Jesus was in danger from the start, that the shadow
of the cross lay over his whole ministry."

It must have sounded like a fair ground. In the outer
precincts of the temple, money changers, the unavoidable and
indispensable *sarrâf* of every Near and Middle Eastern bazaar,
weighed the disparate moneys of the pilgrims, Hellenistic and
Roman coins stanmped with pagan emblems, worn out by long
usage or unscrupulously filed off, in exchange for Jewish
shekels, legal tender for temple taxes and fees. Herdsmen
drove bellowing oxen, bleating kids and lambs for burnt- and
peace-offerings. Folks of little means, who could not afford
expensive victims, bargained for pigeons and doves, all shout-
ing, wrangling and cursing, a scene à la Brueghel. Outraged,
the young pilgrim from Nazareth "made a whip out of cords
and drove them all, with their sheep and oxen, out of the
temple, poured out the coins of the changers and overturned
their tables"; and commanded the venders of pigeons to "take
away their cages" (John 2:14-16), for "is it not written, My
house shall be a house of prayer for all peoples, but you have
made it a den of thieves" (Mk 11:17) or, in John 2:16, "a
market-place", οἶκος ἐμπορίου, echoing an oracle of Zeka-
riah 14:21, "In that day, there will no longer be merchants in
the temple". Jesus would hardly have found it necessary to
appeal to Scripture for condemning the sacrilegeous disorder
which aroused him. It was nothing new. Nehemiah had to
throw out of the temple, with "all his household furniture",
a certain Tobiah who, with the connivance of the priest Elia-
shib, had simply moved "into a large chamber previously used

for the storage of offerings, frankincense, vessels and the tithes of grain, wine and oil" (Neh 13:4-9). Housing must have been scarce in post-exilic Jerusalem!

Jesus' quotation from the prophets, unanimously reported by the four evangelists, conveys much more than a condemnation of incongruous misuse or riotous commotion in the temple courts. The text of Isaiah envisions a new order of things in an indefinite future: "The foreigners who join themselves to the Lord ... I will bring to my holy mountain and make them joyful in my house of prayer". Jeremiah, who had never been overawed by the Jews' hypocritical appeal to the inviolability of the temple — "the temple of the Lord! the temple of the Lord! the temple of the Lord!" (Jer 7:4) — threatens that it may well go down like the sanctuary of Shiloh, "where I made my name dwell at first, says the Lord" (7:11-14). And Jesus, upholding the sanctity of his Father's house, hints unambiguously at his sonship and his messianic mission, of which he has been conscious since childhood: "Did you not know that I must be in my Father's house?" (Luke 2:49)[5] The disciples, witnesses of the expulsion of the merchants and the changers, remembered later that it was written: "Zeal for thy house will consume me", a messianic prophecy from the Psalmist (John 2:17, quoting from Psalm 69:9 RSV).[6]

A distinctive feature of the Fourth Gospel is the use of the prophetic mode to report the various elements of the pericopes and related fragments common to the four Gospels but differently organized: the Master's teaching and healing in the temple, the awe of the disciples at the sight of the temple battlements, the Jews inquiring by which authority did Jesus do "these things"? It was not for John a question of legal authority, ἐξουσία, but a sign, σημεῖον, which would authenticate Jesus' prediction of the messianic age which he came to usher (John 2:18-22). The Jews asked for a sign; a chain of signs is given to them, each one confirming the

---

[5] Or, "about my Father's business", KJ, following the Greek.

[6] Or, "has eaten me up" KJ, the so-called "prophetic perfect" of the Hebrew grammars.

preceding one.[7] At short range, the death and the resurrection
of Jesus, for when he spoke of the destruction of the temple,
"he meant the temple of his body" (verse 21); this the disciples remembered later. After some three decades, Jerusalem
would be destroyed and of the temple itself there would not
be left standing a stone upon a stone (Matthew 24:2, Mark
13:2; Luke 19:44; 21:6). Jesus had predicted the catastrophe,
sitting with the disciples opposite the temple, in the shade of
an olive tree (Matthew 24:3). The first two links of the chain
point to the final reality of the new order announced by the
prophets, when the risen Lord himself would sit in judgment
and when "the first heaven and the first earth" would have
receded before the new creation which the seer of Patmos was
given to behold (Revelation 21:1).

Whether the entire episode is at its original place in the
Fourth Gospel, in the early phase of Jesus' public activity, or
whether this dating results from an accidental or intentional
transposition, is immaterial to our purpose. In any case, the
message is the announcement of a new economy of salvation
inaugurated by the Lord Jesus. For the Synoptics it is a summary of the doctrine implicitly or explicitly taught by the
Master. For St. John, it is a program which will be realized
step by step, day after day. Whether a summary or a program,
the substance of the message is the same.

The nocturnal visit of Nicodemus, an influential member
of the βουλή, the Jewish *Sanhedrin*, and the discourse on
the new life in the Spirit (John 3:1-21), follow after the
episode of the merchants driven out of the temple. Eager to
justify his chronological arrangement over against that of
the Synoptics, the author of the Fourth Gospel notes expressly
that Nicodemus, the Pharisee who warned his fellow Sanhedrites against condemning a man without a hearing (John
7:50-51) and who later would help Joseph of Arimathaea
preparing the body of the Crucified for burial (John 19:39-
40), was that Nicodemus who, some two years earlier, had
secretly visited the Master. He wanted to see and hear for

---

[7] Similar strings of prophecies appear in Luke's account of the meeting in
the temple, cf. ch. 5.

himself, and form his own opinion of the man, a controversial Nazarene who went roving through the land, healing the sick and preaching novelties among inflammable Galileans who bore impatiently the rule of the Romans, their puppet princelings and petty officials, who were most suspicious of the politicians of the capital and had little use for the niceties of the temple's theologians or casuists.

Nicodemus was no hero, no coward either, above all desirous not to compromise his authority by rashly taking sides; at the time of his meeting with Jesus, a typical Pharisee, literal and legalistic. The opposition between two ideologies is clearcut; it does not yet show the fierce aggressiveness which will flare up later and blur the issues. The Jewish way of life, based on the material observance of the Law of Moses and aggravated by the minute precepts of the canonists, had become a dead letter; the new order would demand that a man be born from above (ἄνωθεν) or, as the translations have it, be born again. Now this was beyond the grasp of Nicodemus, who wondered how on earth a man could be born anew: "Can he enter a second time into his mother's womb and be born?", a preposterous question, as inane as the question of the Jews after the multiplication of the loaves. When Jesus declared that the bread he would give for the life of the world was his own flesh, they wondered how "that man" could give his flesh to be eaten (John 6:52). New life in the new age which Jesus came to inaugurate is the fruit of the Spirit, and "the Spirit blows where it chooses to blow" (John 3:8).[8] Nicodemus' literalism had thus far hampered the divine breeze which was to blow in force on the morning of Pentecost "that it might renew the face of the earth", as a responsorium of the Latin breviary has it. The conversation with Christ and the vision of the Crucified would gradually awaken our Pharisee from his torpor.

The discourse ends by shifting from the theme of life to the theme of light: entrance into the life in the Spirit is through Christian baptism, which St. Paul and the Fathers call an "illumination", φωτισμός, for the Christian is enlightened once and for all, ἅπαξ φωτισθέντας, that he may become par-

[8] Greek, τὸ πνεῦμα ὅπου θέλει πνεῖ; Vulgate, *spiritus ubi vult spirat.*

taker of the Holy Spirit (Hebr 6:4). The letter to the Ephe-
sians (5:14) quotes what seems to be a fragment of an ancient baptismal hymn:

> Arise, O thou who sleepest.
> Arise from among the dead,
> And Christ shall shine upon thee.

Thus the discourse on the new life winds up as a baptismal
homily. In like manner, the discourse on the Living Bread
will connote the eucharist. Let us add this: baptism confers
no legal status which would supplant the Mosaic institution.
But we are given "the earnest of the Spirit" (2 Cor 5:5) and
ushered into a world order which has Creation itself for its
charter, in order that, being made in the image of God and
being delivered from our sins, we may grow into his likeness
and be made partakers of the life and blessedness of the
divine persons.

THE PARALYTIC AT THE POOL. The miraculous
healing of a paralytic at the pool of *Bethzatha* (John 5:1-18)
and the discourse on the works which should accredit Jesus
as Son of God and Messiah (5:19-47) is dated by the author
of the Fourth Gospel from "a feast of the Jews", unspecified.
Jesus had left the capital after the tumultuous expulsion of
the merchants from the temple and after his nocturnal inter-
view with Nicodemus. He spent the interval of time between
the passover reported by John 2:13 and the anonymous feast
of 5:1 travelling through the land: first down to the lower
tract of the Jordan valley, where John the Baptist had witnessed to his divine identity and messianic mission; then
through Samaria, where he conversed with the woman of
Sychar at the well of Jacob; and finally to Galilee, where he
healed the son of a royal official (John 4:46-54, cf. Mtt 8:5-
13 and Lk 7:2-10). This is how we find him next on his way
up to Jerusalem to attend the unnamed feast of John 5:1.
These topographical indications given at random by the evangelists and the seemingly precise topography of the Fourth
Gospel are somewhat disconcerting: too many question-marks

for a good concordance! Where was Jesus baptized by John?
On this side of the Jordan, the traditional site close to the
monastery of the Prodromos, or across the river? Where is
"Aenon near Salim", where John was baptizing, according to
the Fourth Gospel 3:23? [9] And did Jesus himself baptize even
more disciples than John, "although, to tell the truth, it was
not Jesus, but rather his disciples, who baptized" (John 4:1-
2)? An exact reconstitution of Jesus' itineraries is nigh unto
impossible. [10] Is it, after all, necessary? Our purpose is not to
write a guide-book à la Baedeker, nor the biography which
we declared could not be written.

The scene of the miracle was the pool of *Bethzata* or
Bezatha; a variety of other readings are found in the Greek
and the versions: *Belzetha, Bethesda,* and *Bethsaïda.* The pool
was near the Sheep Gate (Nehemiah 3:1, 32), a northern
entrance to the temple area. It is described by the author of the
Fourth Gospel as "having five porticoes"; in other words it
consisted in twin rectangular basins lined with columns and
divided by a median pier, an arrangement which has been
confirmed by archeological exploration. The pool was fed by
an underground spring whose periodic gushing is described
by the evangelist and glossed over by early commentators
whose explanations have been incorporated in the text of a
number of Greek manuscripts and in the Latin Vulgate. A
local belief had it that an angel descended by intervals into
the pool and troubled the water; a crowd of invalids lay waiting in the galleries, for the first one who plunged into the
pool after the motion of the water was sure to be cured. The
turbulence of the water was most likely a phenomenon of
which the spring of *Gihôn* in the valley of the Cedron
(*Qidrôn*) is another example. The water originates underground in a cavern of limestone forming a natural siphon,
and issues forth when reaching a certain level, like at the
fountain of Vaucluse in Provence, celebrated by Petrarca.

Our man had been stricken "thirty-eight years ago"— one

[9] This problem is compounded with the difficulty of identifying the sites
of Bethany beyond Jordan (John 1:28) and of Aenon near Salim (John 3:23).

[10] In spite of brave attempts by modern scholars, like the late G. Dalman,
in his book *Orte und Wege Jesu.*

of those factual notations frequent in the Fourth Gospel and commented artificially by the allegorists. Because he had no one to help him into the pool, another patient always managed to be first, and the poor man lay frustrated, with the others. Seeing this, Jesus ordered him to "rise, take up his pallet and walk", and he was healed on the spot. We are reminded of a similar miracle recorded by the Synoptics. Was it more difficult to make a paralytic walk than to forgive his sins, a divine prerogative which Jesus claims for himself? (Mtt 9:2-8; Mk 2:3-12; Lk5:18-26).

The miracle at the pool and the healing of the paralytic of Capernaum were the response of Christ to the faith-desire of man — not that a prayer of faith should automatically result in its object being granted, for it is not a piece of machinery operating on human initiative, nor a patent remedy to be kept in the medicine cabinet. As for Jesus' admonition to the paralytic of Bethzatha "to sin no more, that nothing worse befall you" (John 5:14), it is not to be explained as if that man had been stricken in punishment for his sins; to be sure, many sinful acts bring about a temporal retribution, but for us to interpret the sore condition of a man as the result of a sin committed by him is tantamount to pronouncing a retroactive judgment on facts unknown or unknowable.

It was on a sabbath that Jesus had healed the paralytic at the pool of Bethzatha, and similarly the paralytic whom they had brought to him at Capernaum; so also a man "possessed of an impure spirit", in the synagogue where Jesus had been teaching, in the early days of his public activity (Mk 1:21-26; Lk 4:31-35). This was grounds enough for holding that peripatetic healer in contempt of the Law, even though extenuating circumstances could be taken into consideration. In his discussions with hostile scribes and Pharisees, Jesus argued both from Scripture and from common sense that the Law suffered exceptions, for "the sabbath was made for man and not man for the sabbath" (Mk 2:27). And some time later Jesus would put the Law in proper perspective: "Did not Moses give you the Law ... and circumcision, and you circumcize a man on the sabbath? Why then are you angry with me because on the sabbath I made a man's body well?"

(John 7:22-23). But Jesus aggravated his case by his indirect, but increasingly clear claim to be the Messiah. Had not the demon exorcized from the lunatic of Capernaum cursed Jesus for being "God's Holy One"? In Jesus' own words, the healer was one greater than Solomon, greater than the temple, Lord of the sabbath (Mtt 12:6, 8, 42; Lk 11:31). St. John concludes his account of the miracle at the pool by noting that "the Jews sought all the more to murder Jesus because he not only broke the sabbath, but also called God his Father, making himself equal to God" (John 5:18).

The discourse on the works of the son answers the double accusation borne against Jesus, that he violated the sabbath and made himself equal to God. God is never idle, he is always in act, he *is* act: "My Father works hitherto, and I am working". The rest of God after the six days of creation, prototype of the Hebrew sabbath (Gen 2:2), does not interrupt the unceasing government of the world through Providence, nor will it stay the course of God's justice toward men, for he is the God "who kills and makes alive", as Hannah sang (1 Sam 2:6). "So also does the Son give life to whom he will, for the Father has given all judgment to the Son ... because he is the Son of man [11]. . . . The hour is coming when all who are in the tombs will hear his voice and come forth ... to the resurrection unto life. . . .or the resurrection unto judgment" (John 5:22, 29).

Three testimonies are brought to uphold Jesus' claim to be master of the sabbath, and the Messiah, Son of God: the testimony of John the Baptist "to whom you [Jews] sent emissaries, and he has borne witness to the truth" (John 5:33); the testimony of Jesus' works, not the works of a man, but the very display of God's own energies, through which the Creator makes himself known to his creatures, "His voice

[11] Moslem Jerusalem folklore attributes to Jesus the role of judge on the last day. The expression "Son of man" is the translation of the Aramaic *bar nashâ* which by itself means nothing more than "a man". Jesus used this title to describe the humility of his present condition or, in an eschatological perspective, his messianic role in the restoration of mankind and the cosmic advent of a new age; cf. Daniel 7:13, and the Jewish apocalyptic writings, Henoch and 4 Esdras.

you have never heard, his form you have never seen, and you do not have his word abiding in you, because you do not believe him whom he has sent" (John 5:37-38); and the testimony of Scripture, which turns against Jesus' accusers and convinces them of spiritual blindness and obstinacy, "for had you believed Moses, you would believe me, since he wrote of me; but if you believe not his writings, how then shall you believe my words?" (John 5:46-47).

THE PASCHA OF THE BREAD OF LIFE. In the year A.D. 29, if we agree on the chronological scheme outlined above,[12] Jesus did not ascend to Jerusalem for the passover. He was by then heavily engaged in a ministry of healing and announcing the "Good News" in Galilee and the district of the lake. The miracle of the multiplication of the loaves is reported unanimously by the Synoptics and the Fourth Gospel; the passover was at hand (John 6:4). No reason is given for Jesus' abstention from the annual pilgrimage; actually the law of attendance suffered exceptions, see above, ch. 5. Or does St. John hint here at the passing of Old Testament figures: the manna of Exodus' days, the sacrifice of the paschal lambs in the temple of Jerusalem, a ritual which had been substituted for the older celebration of the passover by families? These figures foreshadowed the Christian eucharist, whenever and wherever a priest, in the name of Christ, would bless the bread and the wine to make them, through the operation of the Holy Spirit, the body and blood of the Lord Jesus.

The scenario outlined by John 6:1-14 and by the Synoptics (Mtt 14:13-21; Mk 6:31-44; Lk 9:10-17) is deceptively simple. It is repeated in Mtt 15:32-39 and Mk 8:1-9 with insignificant variants. Whether these refer to a similar miracle or represent a second version of the same is immaterial, but one thing is certain: the miracle must have made a deep impression on the masses. Jesus was followed by a crowd of enthusiasts and of curious, "because they saw the signs, σημεῖα, which he did on those who were diseased" (John

---

[12] Whether or not we agree on this chronological scheme is of minimal importance for the deeper meaning of the episode, which transcends historical circumstances.

6:2). The place was in the hills, away from the villages of the lake shore. It was getting late. Would Jesus dismiss them? But "they had followed him for three days, and they had nothing to eat" — "If I send them away hungry to their homes they will faint on the way, and some of them have come from far!" (Mk 8:3). Now a lad had with him five loaves of barley and two fishes, "but what is that for so many?" (John 6:9). Jesus ordered the people to sit on the grass and, as he would be doing one year later, on the eve of the passover, he took the five loaves and the fish, blessed the bread, broke it and gave it to the disciples, so that they could distribute it to the crowd; "and they all ate and were satisfied" (Mtt 14:19). Our liturgical traditions and the iconography of the early church have drawn their formulae and their symbols from the Gospel narratives: the five *prosphorai* of the divine liturgy in the Russian usage, and the loaves and fish of the catacomb paintings with the acronym ΙΧΘΥΣ, "Jesus Christ, Son of God, Savior". Five thousand people were fed, and twelve baskets filled with leftovers. The second version of the miracle gives slightly different figures: seven loaves, four thousand people, and seven baskets — an excellent pretext for allegorical developments! Do not try to imagine the miracle any further than the Gospel descriptions make us see and hear. Magician tricks will not do, even for putting the episode on the screen. Well-meaning preachers explain that Jesus had induced his audience to share whatever small provisions they had by themselves with their neighbors. It is very ingenious, most edifying and ... totally unwarranted. We have to deal here with a mystery of faith, *mysterium fidei*,[13] if we may use the very words which the Roman Church has incorporated into the formula of eucharistic consecration.

The miracle of the loaves has its epilogue in the discourse of Jesus on the bread of life in the synagogue of Capernaum on the following sabbath. The intervening days were spent in sailing to and from the fishing villages of the lake. We gather from the accounts of the Synoptics and the Fourth Gospel that

---

[13] The expression "mystery of faith" used in the Latin *anaphora*, appears in a different context in 1 Timothy 3:9, "Let the deacons keep the mystery of faith in a pure conscience."

Jesus had sent his disciples ahead to wait for him in the region of Bethsaïda, on the north-eastern shore, across the Little Jordan, while he dismissed the crowds; then he would somehow catch up with them. "He went up the mountain by himself to pray" (Mtt 14:22-23; Mk 6:45-46). He was anxious to find some solitude and escape the indiscrete zeal of those who spoke of kidnaping him to make him king (John 6:15). Matthew, Mark and John place in the same night, "during the fourth watch", the episode of Jesus walking over the waves of the lake to join the disciples; they landed first at Gennesareth, and finally at Capernaum, on the Galilean side. All that coming and going disconcerted the crowds and caused them to disperse. It is difficult for us to figure out with topographical precision the report of the evangelists, due to their use of the ambiguous "on the other side", or "across", and to the variants of the text,[14] to which must be added the puzzle of two unidentified quantities in the second recension of the miracle of the loaves: "the region of Magadan" (Mtt 15:39) — would it be Magdala? — and "the district of Dalmanutha" (Mk 8:10).[15]

St. John's record of the discourse on the living bread begins with a lively dialogue between Jesus and the crowd of hearers who finally succeeded in trailing him to Capernaum. The pointed exchange is somewhat smoothed in the rhythmic prose of the Fourth Gospel and in the English versions, especially the King James.

"You seek me, not because you saw signs, but because you ate your fill of the loaves."—"What sign dost thou show us, that we may see, and believe thee? Our fathers ate the manna in the wilderness." — "Indeed, but it is not Moses who gave you the bread from heaven, the bread which gives life to the world."—"Sir, always give us that bread," a prayer halfway between faith and unbelief. Obviously the thought of the Jews

[14] A Byzantine tradition locates this episode on a hill above 'Aïn Tabgha (northwestern shore of the lake) where the remains of a church and a mosaic pavement representing the miracle of the loaves have been discovered; cf. A. M. Schneider, *The Church of the Multiplication of the Loaves and Fishes*, London, 1937.

[15] "Dalmanutha" and "Magadan" (Magdala in the KJ). See F. M. Abel, *Géographie de la Palestine* II, p. 373.

is how to fill their belly. It was time to clear up the misunderstanding. "I am the bread of life; he who comes to me shall not hunger.... I am the bread of life; your fathers ate the manna in the wilderness, and they died. But this is the bread which came down from heaven, that men may eat of it and not die.... and the bread which I give is my flesh, which I give for the life of the world." Voices were heard in the crowd: "How can this man give us his flesh to eat? A hard saying! Who can listen to it?" Jesus was aware that some of the disciples would not believe. They stood on a threshold, and so do we; there is before us a choice of life or death.

The discourse on the bread of life connotes the Christian eucharist, just as the discourse on the new life in the Spirit (John 3:5-21) connoted the mystery of baptism, although the primary object of both is the new economy of salvation as a whole. We may have noticed that in the synagogue of Capernaum, not one word was spoken about the temple, its priesthood, its institutions; these are simply bypassed and abandoned to their destiny. The old economy was provisional and figurative. Jesus had said to the Samaritan woman at the well: "The hour comes when neither on Mount Gerizim nor in Jerusalem will you worship the Father (John 4:21). The passover of the five loaves and the discourse of the living bread belong already in the new age.

THE WEEK OF THE TABERNACLES. The summer months had passed. All Israel was making ready for the autumnal feast of the tabernacles. Jesus' brothers[16] urged him to go up with them to Jerusalem. Jesus hesitated at first and decided not to join them. They had never understood him; he had the gift of healing, he had shown that he could draw crowds after him, and there he sat in the obscurity of Galilean villages among little people instead of manifesting himself in the capital, where the power of his word would move throngs of upper class burghers and pilgrims, and where he had a chance to make himself be recognized as a leader of the nation! Now that is just what Jesus wanted to avoid. He had not

---

[16] The expression "Jesus' brothers" means usually his relatives and kin; in Matthew 28:10, his disciples: "Go and tell my brethren to go to Galilee."

been born to be an earthly ruler, and in a few months he would declare to Pilate that "his kingdom was not of this world."

After his brothers had left, he also went up, by himself, secretly, as it were, ὡς ἐν κρυπτῷ (John 7:10). The incognito could not last; the Jews expected him. "Some said: He is a good man; others: no, he leads the people astray" (7:12). Toward the middle of the feast (7:14), he was teaching in the temple, much to the astonishment of the crowd and to the intense displeasure of the authorities. He was no patented rabbi, and how is it that he dared teach? He even did show some learning, "but how could he know his letters, having not studied?" (7:15).

These questions opened a round of passionate discussions, the movement of which is easily perceived in the Greek text and in those translations which have endeavored to keep the rhythmic form of St. John's recording: the solemn, balanced periods of Jesus' statements, abruptly broken by the staccato of the Jews' attacks, their insidious questioning, and their desultory exclamations. It brings to mind the plain-chant melody of the Gospels of passion week in the ancient monastic usage of the west: the voice of Christ, grave and unadorned, *andante sostenuto*; the recitative of the "evangelist"; the strident dissonance of Judas' voice, and the angry clamor of the crowd.

The debate was about the authority of Jesus' teaching and the source of that authority, when, toward the middle of the feast, he exclaimed: "My doctrine is not mine, but of Him who sent me . . . But you do not know Him! I do, for I come from Him, and He sent me" (John 7:16, 28-29). A daring statement; in the eyes of his enemies, a blasphemy! "So they sought to arrest him, but no one laid his hands on him, because his hour had not come. Yet many of the people believed in him, saying: when the Christ appears, will he do more signs than this man?" (7:30-31). Even the guards, whom the chief priest sent after him, would return without having fulfilled their mandate. "No man, they said, ever taught as this man" (7:32, 45-49).

"This man" claims to be, and is, the Christ, the Messiah, God's anointed. These are not three different titles. The first two have become, so to speak, worn out by a long Christian usage, and we have forgotten their original meaning. "Christ", without the article, has even become a proper name in English parlance. It is in fact the exact rendering of the Hebrew *meshîyah*; the Messiah is more than a special envoy from above. The anointed one is he who bestows the Holy Spirit, and the gift of the Spirit is symbolized by a solemn anointing with consecrated oil, the holy chrism of the Orthodox and the Latins. Thus is Jesus designated as the unique bearer of the eternal Spirit, whom he will send on the day of Pentecost. What St. John proclaims here is not only the divine character of Jesus' mission, but Jesus' divinity.

"On the last day of the feast, the great day, Jesus stood up and shouted: If any one thirst, let him come to me and drink! He who believes in me, as the Scripture says, out of his bosom shall flow rivers of living water" (John 7:37-38; cf. 4:14; Is 55:1, 58:11). By appropriating Isaiah's oracle, Jesus once more declared his identity. Nobody missed the point, neither his enemies nor those who would rally after him. "Now he speaks openly" (John 7:26). "Some said: this is really the prophet! Others said: this is the Christ! But some objected: how can the Christ come from Galilee, since Scripture says that he comes from the house of David, from the town of Bethlehem" (7:40-42).

The ritual procession of sukkoth to the pool of Siloam [17] may have formed the background of the scene described by the evangelist, who notes that "Jesus said this about the Spirit which those who believe in him were to receive, for as yet the Spirit had not been given, because Jesus was not yet glorified" (John 7:39). We have here an outstanding example of St. John's chronological notations given both for historical accuracy in reporting the words and deeds of Jesus, and for theological precision in outlining the general development of our common salvation. It is probably not inappropriate to note here that the liturgical tradition of the Orthodox Church assigns John 7:14-30 and 7:37-52 and 8:12 as Gospel lessons for Mid-Pentecost and Pentecost. [18]

[17] On the temple ritual for the feast of tabernacles, see ch. 4.

[18] G. Barrois, "Scripture Readings for Mid-Pentecost and Pentecost", St. Vladimir's Theological Quarterly 21/3 (1977), pp. 148-159.

The leaders still hoped to trip up Jesus on a legal point, which would enable them to start proceedings against him. St. John notes that the so-to-speak "pre-trial hearing" was held in the room of the temple's treasury. "Thou bearest witness to thyself; thy testimony is not valid."—"And if I bear witness to myself, still my testimony is true, for I know whence I come and whither I go.... It is written in your law that the testimony of two men is true. I bear witness to myself, and the Father who sent me bears witness to me" (John 8:13-14, 17-18). They said to him: "Where is thy father?" — "You neither know me nor my Father; if you knew me, you would know my Father also" (John 8:19). Then, a prophetic word: "When you have lifted up the son of man [on the cross], then will you know that *I am He*" (8:28, cf. verse 24); translated literally from the Greek: "I, I AM". The strange formula echoes distinctly the voice which Moses heard from the midst of the burning bush (Ex 3:6, 14; see above, ch. 2). Here is not the place to start a scholastic argument on the *Ens in se,* the "Being Itself"; we may simply point to the letters inscribed on the nimbus of the Pantocrator on our Byzantine icons: ʽΟ ῀Ων.

Jesus categorical affirmation brings the confrontation to a climax. The Jews boast of being the sons of Abraham. Jesus retorts: "Your father Abraham rejoiced that he was to see my day; he saw it and rejoiced." — "Thou art not fifty years old, and thou hast seen Abraham!" — "Truly I say unto you: before Abraham was, I am" (John 8:56-59). And this is final. Commenting on the words of Jesus, the late Fr. Lagrange remarked that "I am" means in this context more than preexistence, for preexistence connotes time, but "I AM", ἐγώ εἰμι, means absolute existence, without any reference to temporal categories.[19] Jesus is the Son of God and himself God: supreme truth, or pure blasphemy! The Jews picked up stones to hurl at him, but he went through their midst and left the temple area.

THE MAN BORN BLIND. St. John's account of the healing of a man blind from birth and the transcript of Jesus'

---

[19] M. J. Lagrange, *L'Evangile selon Saint Jean* (1925), p. 256.

discourse on the good shepherd (chapters 9 and 10) follow the regular pattern already observed. However, the time-notation permitting us to date the event is not extant in the present condition of the text. We have hinted earlier that the miracle may have occurred during the festival of tabernacles. As they meet the blind man begging for alms, the disciples ask the Master why he was born blind. The prejudice common among the Jews, that such conditions must be in punishment for some sin, baffles them: the man was blind before he could sin! Jesus' answer: "Neither he nor his parents have sinned" (John 9:3). As a matter of fact, Jesus did not answer the "why?", which remains the secret of the Father; but the healing of the blind man had the value of a sign, "that the works of God might become manifest, for we must work (Latin Vulgate: I must work) the works of Him who sent me while it is day, for night is coming" (9:4) — the night of the cross and the tomb!

The description of the miracle is laconic to the extreme: Jesus spits on the ground, makes some mud from the dust, anoints the eyes of the blind man and orders him to "go and wash in the pool of Siloam, which means: *sent*". So he went and washed and came back seeing (9:6-7). The pool of Siloam is the same as the pool of *Shélach* (Neh 3:15) or the "waters of *Shiloach*" (Is 8:6) — the etymology given by the evangelist is correct. The symbolism is evident: Jesus is the one sent by the Father.

The exchange between the Pharisees, irked because the healing happened the sabbath, and the blind man and his parents, strikes a new note. The parents are afraid of the authorities and do not do anything but identify their son, "who will speak for himself; he is of age" (9:21). But he who was blind is not impressed, and finally gives saucy answers to the questions which the Pharisees keep shooting at him: "We know that this man [Jesus] is a sinner." — "Whether he is a sinner, I do not know; one thing I know: I was blind, and now I see." — "How did he open thine eyes?" — "I have told you already, but you would not listen . . . Why do you want to hear it again? Do you want to become his disciples?" That was too much for self-respecting Pharisees to hear: infuriated, "they cast him out", the sanction which all Jews fear.

The conclusion of the episode is, on the part of him who had been healed, a profession of Christian faith. Jesus, having heard that they had cast him out, and having found him, said, "Believest thou in the Son of man?" — "And who is he, sir, that I may believe in him?" — "Thou hast seen him, and it is he who speaks to thee." — "Lord, I believe," and he worshipped him, the Messiah (9:35-38). Jesus said: "For judgment I came into the world, that these who do not see may see, and that those who see become blind," namely those who boast of their superior I.Q. in opposition to those who seek humbly after truth (9:39). This had been an article of the messianic doctrine of the Old Testament prophets, Isaiah, Jeremiah and Ezekiel.

For a transition to the discourse on the good shepherd, St. John notes the reaction of some Pharisees, who happened to be nearby and who had heard — or overheard — the words of Jesus. Their leaders did not appear; their mind was made up anyway. They bided their time for the right moment to proceed legally against the one whom they had already condemned in their private counsels. As for the rank and file of the sect, eager for recognition in the eyes of their superiors through officiousness, they asked: "Are we, the Pharisees, all blind?" Their question gave Jesus the opportunity to take the offensive. His discourse is both a parable and a prophecy (John 10:1-18). The image of the good shepherd had been made familiar by the prophets, in a messianic perspective of which Jesus brings the realization. He is the good shepherd, who leads the sheep into the fold. Others break in "only to steal, and kill, and destroy." The good shepherd gives his life for his flock; "come the wolf, and the hireling takes to flight, for he cares nothing for the sheep". The prophetic conclusion envisions a new order of things, which will transcend and transpose the Old Testament economy of salvation, the observances of the Tôrah and the precepts of the synagogue: "I have other sheep that are not of this fold; I must bring them also and they, too, will heed my voice. So there shall be one fold, one shepherd" (John 10:16).

Next, we find Jesus in Jerusalem for the feast of the dedication of the temple, the *hanukkah*, with a crowd of Jews and pilgrims, under the portico of Solomon (John 10:22-38); it must have been in the winter of A.D. 29. No miracle this time. The account given by the author of the Fourth Gospel reads like an epitome of Jesus' previous discussions with the Jews in the temple. The lines were sharply drawn. For his enemies, he was a character of doubtful origin, a Nazarene, but "can anything good come out of Nazareth?" (John 1:46); a carpenter by trade, who had left his shop and now roved about the land as a professional healer and preacher of novelties. His partisans, whose number fluctuated with the winds of public opinion, were impressed by his cures and stood half-convinced by his preaching, or was he, after all, nothing more than a successful charlatan? For the leaders, he was a violator of the sabbath and contemner of the Mosaic institutions, a trouble-maker and would-be revolutionist — Galilee was teeming with such zealots! — a self-proclaimed Messiah, claiming to be the Son of God and making himself equal to God! The crowd remembered his parable of the good shepherd which he had applied to himself during the feast of tabernacles, and now, challenged by the Jews, he brazenly re-affirmed his claims. That was too much; the mob would not stop short of stoning him, the traditional punishment for those convicted of blasphemy. "Not because of thy good works do we lapidate thee, but because thou, a man, makest thee God" (John 10:33). They had already picked up stones when Jesus escaped from their hands. He left Jerusalem and "went again across the Jordan", in the place where John at first baptized, and there he remained" (John 10:40). Transjordan had often been a place of refuge for political exiles. Jesus could remember his ancestor David fleeing the revolt of Absalom and being welcomed by Shobi son of Nahash, an Ammonite; Machir, a tribesman from East Manasseh; and Barzillaï, an Aramaean from Gilead (2 Sam 17:27-29).

Jesus, in the brief course of his public life, had gone up

to Jerusalem as a pilgrim. He professed now to be the master of the temple. His death on the cross and his resurrection would establish his reign, and the temple would soon crumble in the fire set by the torch of an unknown Roman soldier.

CHAPTER SEVEN

The Week of the Passion

CHRONOLOGICAL DATA. In the preceding chapter, we left Jesus and the apostles in the region of the Jordan, where they sought a temporary relief from the turbulence of the Jerusalem crowds (John 10:40). We now find them on their way to the capital, in early spring. Both the Fourth Gospel and the Synoptics mention their journey, yet the accounts cannot be harmonized. For the Synoptics, the proximity of the passover was the reason for the journey, and they quote Jesus' words, announcing for the third time that he was going to be delivered to the Gentiles, how they would kill him and how he would rise from the dead on the third day, "but they understood none of these things," notes Luke. The Synoptics show Jesus approaching Jericho, where he healed a blind man, or according to Matthew, "two blind men" (Mtt 20:17-19, 30-34; Mk 10:32-33, 46-52; Lk 18:31-34, 35-43), and received the spontaneous homage of Zacchaeus, the repentant publican (Lk 19:1-10).

According to St. John, Jesus and the apostles set out on their journey upon hearing from a messenger of the severe illness of his friend Lazarus, the brother of Martha and Mary of Bethany, a locality near Jerusalem. St. John notes pointedly that "Jesus tarried two days longer at the place where he was" (John 11:1-6). On arriving at Bethany, he found Lazarus dead and buried for four days; he had the tomb opened and called the dead man back to life (John 11:11-44). In view of the reactions of the crowd and the hostile designs of the Jewish leaders, Jesus left for a place called Ephraim, where he stayed for a while with the disciples (John 11:54).[1] The

[1] Ephraïm, St. John's transcription of the ancient 'Ophra (1 Sam 13:17), a village some fifteen miles northeast of Jerusalem, at the limit between the

account of the miracle is unique to the Fourth Gospel, where it is treated as an independent unit, forming a sort of preface for the history of the passion.

From then on, the four evangelists concur on the events of the week, granting a few transpositions of episodes, due to their particular methods of exposition: the Synoptics proceeding by topical units, while St. John intends to present the facts in their actual sequence, and shows himself concerned with the doctrinal significance of the facts.

We may now outline the calendar of "Great and Holy Week", keeping in mind that the days were counted, *for liturgical purposes*, from sunset to sunset, so that the passover meal, *sêder*, and the unleavened bread, *matsoth*, were eaten on the evening of the fourteenth day of *Nîsân*, already reckoned as the fifteenth. Furthermore, in the year that Jesus died, the day of passover, fifteenth of Nîsân, was a sabbath.[2]

a) "Six days before passover", a supper at Bethany. Mary, the sister of Lazarus and Martha, anoints the feet of Jesus, who had returned from Ephraïm (John 12:1-9). It must have been on saturday night, eighth of Nîsân, counting back from the day of the passover meal. The other time-notation of the Gospels during passion week will be reckoned in the same manner. The supper at Bethany is related in Matthew 26:6-13 and Mark 14:3-9, with minor differences: the date is not given, nor is Mary mentioned by name.

b) "The next day", sunday, ninth of Nîsân, the messianic entrance of Jesus into Jerusalem, "Palm Sunday", (John 12: 12-15); same episode, without indication of date, in Matthew 21:1-11; Mark 11:1-10; Luke 19:29-38.

c) "Jesus said to the disciples: You know that after two

---

cultivated zone of the Palestinian highlands and the barren hills sloping steeply down to the depression of the Jordan; a mountain road leads to the oasis of Jericho via 'Aïn Duq. The old name, 'Ophra ,because of its consonance with the Arabic *'Afrît*, a she-devil (radical *'a-f-r*), was changed into *Tayibet el-'Ism*, "propitious is the name", or simply *Tayibeh*. See F. M. Abel, *Géographie de la Palestine* II, pp. 318 and 402.

[2] It has been established that the passover fell on a sabbath in A.D. 30 and 33. Either of these dates can be chosen for dating the death and resurrection of Christ, taking into account two variables: the estimated duration of his public life, and the date of his baptism by John, in the early months of A.D. 28 or 29, when he is said to have been "about" thirty years of age.

days, it is passover, and the Son of man will be delivered up to be crucified" (Mtt 26:2-5; Mk 14:1-2); it was therefore Wednesday, twelfth of *Nîsân*. The chief priests and the scribes conspire to have Jesus kidnaped and put to death, but "not during the feast, lest there be a tumult among the people".

d) "The first day of the unleavened bread, *matsoth*", last supper and institution of the eucharist, on Thursday, thirteenth of *Nîsân* (Mtt 26:17-29; Mk 14:12-25; Lk 22:7-23). The difficulty arising from the remark of Mark and Luke that it was the day of the immolation of the lambs in the temple — normally on the evening of the fourteenth of *Nîsân* — may be explained by assuming that the lambs could be immolated already on the thirteenth when passover fell on the sabbath. Rabbinical speculations, much debated, might authorize this assumption.

e) After supper, during the night of the thirteenth to the fourteenth of *Nîsân*, the vigil in the olive grove of Gethsemane; Jesus is arrested and led to the highpriest; Peter denies his master (Mtt 26:30-75; Mk 14:26-72; Lk 22:39-62; John 18:1-27).

f) On the Friday morning, fourteenth of *Nîsân*, judgment and condemnation of Jesus. The crucifixion at the "third hour", i.e. 9:00 A.M., (Mk 15:25). Darkness "over all the land", from the sixth hour, 12:00 noon, to the ninth hour, 3:00 P.M., when Jesus expires (Mtt 27:45-50; Mk 15:33-37; Lk 23:44-46). Joseph of Arimathea and Nicodemus obtain the body from Pilate and lay it in the tomb after a summary embalming, before sunset, lest the coming sabbath be defiled by the presence of a corpse (Mtt 27:57-60; Mk 15:42-46; Lk 23: 50-56; John 19: 38-42).

g) On the same Friday evening, fourteenth of *Nîsân*, the passover meal of the Jews; on the fifteenth the "great sabbath".

h) On the Sunday, sixteenth of *Nîsân*, before dawn, the tomb is found empty by the myrrh-bearing women and the apostles.

A mere glance at the above summary reveals a serious discrepancy between the Fourth Gospel and the Synoptics.

On the one hand, the Synoptics state that the eucharist was instituted on Thursday, the thirteenth of *Nîsân*, in the course of the passover meal (*sêder*) of Jesus and the twelve, or in immediate relation to it. On the other hand, the four evangelists concur on the celebration of the passover meal of the Jews on Friday, the fourteenth of *Nîsân* after sunset, and of passover day on Saturday, the great sabbath, *Nîsân* 15.

We find ourselves in a dilemma. Perhaps the supper in the upper room did not have the character of the passover meal, a theory formally developed by Dom Calmet, a seventeenth-century Benedictine scholar. The Synoptics have manifestly insisted on whatever was relative to the institution of the eucharist; are we to overlook that, according to them, Jesus and the apostles intended their supper to be the passover meal? It has been argued that the institution of the eucharist, as reported by the Synoptics, shows some affinity with the Jewish *Qiddush*, a blessing over the bread and wine of the sabbath, indeed more than with the ritual of the *sêder* meal, but it is rather questionable to challenge the testimony of the Synoptics in the name of a later practise of rabbinical Judaism.

Or had Jesus decided to eat the passover meal by anticipation, on the Thursday, thirteenth of *Nîsân*, one day before the regular date? But he is not likely to have done this on his own initiative; anyhow, it did not raise any comments on the part of those who witnessed it. There is no certain evidence for other examples of the *sêder* meal being anticipated by private groups or parts of the population, but the hypothesis ought not to be excluded. The fact that passover could fall on a sabbath, joined to the influx of pilgrims from the province or from the diaspora, did not facilitate the exact observance of the rubrics. The Mishnah refers to discussions among the rabbis whether it was permissible to anticipate the immolation of the lambs, in which circumstances and by how long. After all, the passover had been originally a family affair, until it was monopolized by the Jerusalem college of priests. Furthermore divergences due to local customs were to be expected; the Galileans had never been quite *kôsher*! And we must count with the vagaries of time-reckoning by way of visual observation of the waxing and waning of the moon and

with the empirical methods kept through liturgical archaism
for determining the date of passover and proclaiming it
throughout the land. In those conditions, irregularities in
fixing the date of the celebration should not surprise us.[3]

Our chronological essay, to a large extent conjectural, is
intended solely as a guide into the history of the passion, an
aide to the "Twelve Gospels" which we hear on Great and
Holy Thursday; for our aim is not to give a complete account
of the last days of Jesus — an impossible task — but rather
to reach, beneath the tragic episodes of the passion, the essence of the Christian mystery: the human predicament of the
of the Son of God, his divinity obscured until the morning of
the resurrection. We cannot be satisfied with an arianizing
version of the so-called "Jesus of history". His parables and
prophecies unfold under the eyes of our faith the perspective
of the kingdom for whose coming we pray daily, the "new
heaven and the new earth" which it was given to John to con-
template in his solitude of Patmos.

BETHANY (Βηθανία), was the theater of two Gospel
episodes: the raising of Lazarus, and the anointing of Jesus'
feet by his sister Mary, a week before the crucifixion. The name
of the place is a Greek transcription of the Hebrew [Beth]
'Ananiah, a little suburban town some two miles from the
capital, re-settled after the Exile by some Benjaminites (Nehemiah 11:32). It stood on the eastern slope of the Mount
of Olives, up from the modern village of *el-'Azarieh* built
along the road of Jerusalem to Jericho; it keeps up the memory
of the miracle and of the very name of Lazarus. The so-called
"tomb of Lazarus", close to the ruins of a fourth-century
church utterly destroyed, may be authentic. At a short distance
of *el-'Azarieh* down the Jericho road, a Greek church marks
the traditional place where Martha came to meet Jesus and
told him that her brother had died. Village youngsters show

---

[3] Several hypotheses have been advanced for reconstituting the chronology
of passion week on the basis of sectarian calendars. These theories are mentioned and criticized in the book of V. Kesich, *The Gospel Image of Christ*
(St. Vladimir's Seminary Press, 1972), pp. 57-59.

nearby a round-shaped rock supposedly representing Lazarus' donkey.

The episode of the raising of Lazarus is anique to the Fourth Gospel (John 11:1-44). *Dramatis personae:* Lazarus himself, who is mentioned nowhere else in the Gospels; his sisters Martha and Mary, already known to us by a passage of Luke 10:38-42, describing how Martha bustled about, preparing a meal for their guest Jesus, while Mary sat lovingly at his feet; it must have been in the course of one of his ascents to Jerusalem on the occasion of some Jewish festivals, but the place and the time are not mentioned. The psychology of the two sisters, vividly sketched by Luke, will be consistent throughout the entire Gospel records, Synoptics and the Fourth Gospel alike.

On hearing of Jesus' arrival, Martha hurried to meet him. "Lord, if thou hadst been here, my brother would not have died." Crushed by her bereavement, Mary stayed home. Now Martha prays for a miracle, but that is of course impossible! She shared in the ideas of many Jews of her time who believed in a general resurrection on the last day — a theoretical, distant and impersonal conviction. Jesus challenges her faith: "I am the resurrection and the life ... whoever lives and believes in me shall never die; believest thou this?" — "Yes Lord, I believe that thou art the Christ, the son of the Living God!" Mary, overcome by grief, could not even pray; she hoped!

St. John's account of the miracle displays the mystery of Christ's dual nature in its fulness. At the grave, the general emotion got hold of him. He wept, as he would weep over Jerusalem and over the impending disaster of his nation. He was disturbed, like one who loses control over his own reactions. His tears were real tears, not a make-believe show covering a supra-human impassibility. "See how he loved him!" said the Jews. The divine virtue radiating from the person of Jesus is apparent in every detail of the Gospel account. The miracle itself makes it evident, even though we are less inclined than our fathers to establish our faith in the divinity and the sonship of Christ on the basis of miracles.

As is usually the case in the Fourth Gospel, concrete notations reveal, under the picturesque and the circumstantial, a background ignored or deliberately negated by radical criticism. At the grave, Jesus speaks with the authority of one who has a unique mission to fulfill, and challenges the doubters: "Take away the stone! ... Did not I tell you that you would see the glory of God?" To his Father: "I thank thee that thou hast heard me. ... but I have spoken because of the people ... that they may believe that thou hast sent me." To the dead man, a word of command: "Lazarus, come out!" And an order to the bystanders: "Unbind him, and let him go!" The bandages, κειρίαι, *institae*, and the face-cloth, σουδάριον, *sudarium*, with which Lazarus had been laid in the tomb, direct our thoughts to those which pious hands would prepare for the burial of the dead Christ; Peter and John would find the grave-cloths in the empty sepulcher, and the *sudarium* "folded up in a place by itself" (John 20:6-7).

The miracle stirred up conflicting reactions among the populace of Jerusalem. "Many Jews believed ... but some of them went to the Pharisees and reported what Jesus had done." Their leaders, greatly alarmed, "took counsel how to put him to death" (John 11:45-53). Jesus, unsafe in the city, and because his hour had not come, felt it prudent to disappear for a while. St. John, who noted with precision the times and places of the last weeks of Jesus, is alone to mention his retreat to Ephraïm (John 11:54).

Those who deny the historicity of the Fourth Gospel regard the raising of Lazarus and the episodes of several persons of the Old and the New Testament being called back to life [4] as legends destined to enhance the glory of the wonderworker and to symbolize the power of God over life and death. This does not explain the silence of the Synoptics on an event which, according to the Fourth Gospel, had set all Jerusalem in commotion. In fact, the Fourth Gospel, written some thirty

[4] For example, the miracles performed by Elijah (Elias) and Elisha (Elisaeus) (1 Kings 17:17-23 and 2 Kings 4:18-37); the raising of the daughter of Jaïrus, still lying on her death-bed (Mtt 9:18, 23-26; Mk 5:22-23, 35-43; Lk 8:41-42, 49-56); the raising of the son of a widow of Naïn, as he was carried out to the grave (Lk 7:11-15), whereas Lazarus was called back to life the fourth day after his burial; also the raising of Tabitha-Dorcas (Acts 9:36-42).

years later than the Synoptics, records many episodes not extant in the Synoptics, which it draws from St. John's personal recollections or from independent sources unknown to the other Evangelists. Is it, then, that Peter, on whose testimony the tradition of the Synoptics was based, had not been present at the grave-side of Lazarus, or had special reasons for not reporting the miracle? — a not very likely hypothesis advanced by the late Fr. Lagrange, who tried to show that there was no place for an account of the raising of Lazarus in the catechesis of the early Christians.[5] There is no real answer to these questions, and here is not the place to speculate on problems of apologetics and of interpretation which do not belong properly within the scope of the present study.

In contrast with the raising of Lazarus reported only by St. John, the episode of the festive supper at Bethany, and of Jesus being anointed with precious nard in prevision of his death and burial, is extant in triplicate (Mtt 26:6-13; Mk 14:3-9; John 12:1-8). Luke's story of a woman of ill repute anointing the feet of Jesus presents great similarities with the Bethany episode, but in a totally different context (Lk 7:36-50).

The supper at Bethany is described with the customary precision of St. John: six days before passover; hence, it may be regarded as the first noteworthy event of the week. It did not follow immediately after the raising of Lazarus; apparently there had been a time-lag between the two episodes. After the miracle at the tomb of Lazarus, Jesus had repaired to Ephraïm in order to avoid the reactions of the crowd. We find him back now for the solemnities of passover; the Jews had been wondering whether he would dare to appear (John 11:56). He may have walked the fifteen miles from Ephraïm to Bethany, or he may have detoured via Jericho and then up the Jerusalem road, as Lagrange suggests;[6] but why this much longer and strenuous journey?

He came to Bethany where they offered him supper. Lazarus was among the guests. Martha was serving, as in the

    [5] L'Evangile de Jésus Christ (1928), pp. 408-409.
    [6] M. J. Lagrange, L'Évangile selon Saint Jean, p. 311.

story of Luke 10:38-42. Mary, carrying a flask of pure nard, anointed Jesus' feet and wiped them with her hair. Judas, one of the twelve, comments sourly: "What a waste! One might have sold the perfume for three hundred dinars and given that to the poor!" He did not care too much about the poor, comments St. John, but he was a thief, κλέπτης, and as he was in charge of the money-box, he "lifted" what was put in it, ἐβάστασεν, a euphemism for "he stole". "Let her alone," replied Jesus, "she meant this in view of my own burial" (John 12:7).[7] From now on, the vision of the cross will dominate the human consciousness of Jesus. Differences between the narratives of John, Matthew and Mark are minimal. According to Matthew and Mark, the supper had been served in the house of Simon "the leper", not, as one might imagine, in the house of Martha. The woman is not identified by name in Matthew and Mark; she poured the perfume on the head of Jesus, not on his feet. But it is, without any doubt, the same story we are reading.

Similarities between the story told by Luke 7:36-50 and the episode of the supper at Bethany as reported by John, Matthew and Mark are undeniable. In Luke, the woman anoints Jesus' feet, as in John; the name of the host is Simon, as in Matthew and Mark, perhaps a coincidence, for the name Simon appears frequently on documents of the time. But the circumstances are different. The scene is in Galilee. Simon, the host, is a Pharisee, eager to see for himself who was that wonderworker of whom everybody talked. The anonymous woman is said to be a sinner of ill repute in the locality, and Luke does not fail to note the *in petto* reflexion of Simon: "If that man were a prophet, he would know who and what sort of creature this is who touches him!" But Jesus had already read through the secret thought of the Pharisee. He proposed a parable: of two insolvent debtors, of whom one owed five hundred *denarii* and the other fifty, and who were both totally forgiven by their generous creditor — "which one

---

[7] Our own translation, based on a well attested sense of the Greek τηρέω "to keep", by derivation: "to keep watch in anticipation of a future happening". Thucydides: "watching for [the opportunity of] a stormy night".

of the two will love him more?" Simon answered: "The one
to whom he forgave more." Right! But, lest the point be
missed, Jesus compared the woman's excess of repentance and
devotion with the cold correctness of the host and concluded:
"Therefore, I tell you, her sins, which are many, are forgiven,"
and, turning to the woman: "Thy sins are forgiven." The
reaction of the bystanders was one of wonderment: "Who is
this, who even forgives sins?"

Reading the story of Luke as an independent unit, we have
the strong impression of a composite piece, in the spirit of
the Synoptic Gospels. Luke may have known the episode of
the anointing from Mark and Matthew, and probably also from
John's tradition, unwritten as yet. But instead of relating the
Bethany episode to the passion as a prophetic gesture, he may
have severed it from the original context and adapted it to
a different set-up, namely that of the Galilean ministry, together with episodes in which Jesus, by demonstrating his
divine power to forgive sins, incurred the suspicion and hostility of the Pharisees. The liberties which Luke took repeatedly
with the order of Mark or of Matthew to compose his Gospel
according to his own scope and method seems to authorize our
hypothesis.

The identity of the woman who anointed Jesus has been
the object of many discussions in the Christian Church. We
cannot speak of traditions proper, still less of the Tradition,
the Παράδοσις, but rather of interpretations, at time pas-
sionately debated, among Christian writers. In general the
Greeks chose to read each pericope for itself, without being
preoccupied overmuch with the identity of the woman. In the
Latin West, the tendency was to regard as one and the same
person the anonymous woman of Matthew and Mark, Mary
of Bethany, sister of Martha and Lazarus, the sinful woman
of Luke, and Mary of Magdala, who had been delivered from
seven devils (Lk 8:2) and who was first to see the risen Christ
(John 20:14-16). These uncritical identifications were discussed by some scholars, for instance Faber Stapulensis (Jac-
ques Lefèvre d'Etaples) in the fifteenth century; but academ-
ism did not prevail over sentimentality. Popular legends of
the exodus of Lazarus and his sisters, combined with the

myrrh-bearing women, are at the origin of local sanctuaries
in Provence and the south of France: *Les Saintes Maries de la
mer*, an isolated fortress church on the Mediterranean shore,
frequented by the gypsies; *la Sainte Baulme*, theater of the
heroic mortifications of Mary Magdalene; the stories, of a
more than doubtful orthodoxy, of Martha's *Tarasque*, a mon-
ster haunting the lower Rhône valley, *la Madeleine* of Véze-
lay in Burgundy, and many others. According to a tradition,
more sober, of the Orthodox East, Mary of Magdala followed
St. John and the Theotokos to Ephesus.

THE MESSIANIC ENTRANCE ON PALM SUNDAY.
The re-appearance of Jesus after his retreat at Ephraïm is described by the four evangelists, who give to their account the
character of a solemn grand entrance (Mtt 21:1-11; Mk
11:1-10; Lk 19:29-40; John 12:12-19). They are unanimous
in reporting the facts, but John alone dates the event: the day
following the supper at Bethany, where Jesus passed the
night.[8] Jesus sent two of his disciples to the hamlet of Bethphage, about half-way from Bethany to the crest of the Mount
of Olives, and instructed them to borrow the colt of an ass
which they would find tethered at the entrance of a certain
courtyard; they should bring it back to him, that he might ride
the two miles separating Bethany from the city. A throng of
local people having learned of his return and, notes John,
pilgrims who had come up for the feast, went out to meet
him.[9] They strewed greenery on the path, holding palms, singing hymns, and acclaiming the wonderworker who had raised
Lazarus from the dead, in whom they recognized their Messiah: "Hosanna! Blessed is he who comes in the name of the
Lord, even the king of Israel!" The acclamation is from Psalm
118:26, a processional hymn for tabernacles (*sukkoth*). The

[8] The order of the pericopes is different in the Synoptics, which follow
each one its own plan, whereas the Fourth Gospel intends to proceed chrono-
logically.

[9] The Mishnah (*Bikkurim* 3:3) relates how the people of Jerusalem went
out to welcome their relatives from the province bringing their tithes for the
feast of tabernacles. This joyful occasion has little in common, except for the
greenery and the singing of hymns, with the improvised manifestation of
Palm Sunday, whose character is definitely messianic.

Christian Church has incorporated it in the eucharistic *ana-phora* after the threefold "Αγιος, "Holy, holy, holy", or, in the Latin liturgy, at the *Sanctus*, when the celebrants cross themselves before the prayers of the *canon missae*. The four evangelists concur in interpreting the scene as the fulfillment of a prophecy of Zechariah (9:9), "as it is written: Fear not, daughter of Zion; behold, thy king is coming, sitting on an ass's colt."

The messianic significance of the episode is clear. St. John remarks that the disciples did not fully understand it at first, "not until Jesus was glorified; only then did they remember that which had been written of him" (John 12:16). But from the very beginning Jesus intended to declare himself as he who was to come. He could have walked from Bethany to Jerusalem — he did it in other instances — but this time he chose to ride, that the Scripture from Zechariah might be fulfilled. The commission given to the two disciples is in some way reminiscent of the signs given to Saul, when he was searching for the lost asses of Kish his father (1 Sam ch. 9 and 10). Or are we to understand that Jesus knew the owner of the little donkey and sent the disciples ahead without further explanations? At any rate a *mise-en-scène*, in order to impress them, is to be excluded, as unworthy of the Master.

St. John notes that the reason for the popular agitation had been the raising of Lazarus. Everybody wanted to see him and to see the wonderworker. Their brand of messianism, politically tainted and which alarmed — rightly — the religious leaders, was not the messianism of the prophets, for whom the King-Messiah would come and conquer, not by a warlike display, for the prophets had always been wary of the military, but solely in the name and virtue of Yahweh.

The verses of the Fourth Gospel following the description of the procession of palms (John 12:20-30) do more than confirm Jesus' messianic claim. He is more than a prophet of the kingdom to come, more than a special human envoy. When some Greek foreigners, moved by curiosity, asked the apostles to see Jesus, he affirmed his sonship, at the very moment when, as a man, he was troubled in his soul and prayed: "Father, save me from this hour! But no! For this purpose

I have come to this hour; Father, glorify thy name!" Then a
voice came from heaven: "I have glorified it, and I will glorify thy name!" Then a voice came from heaven: "I have
glorified it, and I will glorify it again." And the voice was
"for our sake"; we had heard it twice before: when Jesus
was baptized in the Jordan (Mtt 3:17; Mk 1:11; Lk 3:22),
and when he was transfigured on the mountain (Mtt 17:5;
Mk 9:7; Lk 9:35; 2 Peter 1:17-18): "This is my beloved son,
in whom I am well pleased; my son, my chosen one; listen
to him!"

Whereas the Synoptics describe the expulsion of the merchants from the temple immediately after the procession of
palms (Mtt 21:12-13; Mk 11:15-17; Lk 19:45-46), the Fourth
Gospel places the tumultuous scene at the very beginning of
Jesus' public life (John 2:13-17; see above, ch. 6) in order
to mark that, from the very beginning of his Galilean ministry,
he would be a sign of contradiction among his people,
and that the vision of the cross would from then on loom
ominously on the horizon. The doctrinal intent of the Fourth
Gospel ought not to be opposed to the historical character of
the Synoptics as contradictory; still less may the Fourth Gospel
be regarded as a collection of late theologoumena. St. John
would have missed his goal indeed, had he built a "thesis"
on anything else but a reliable factual basis!

PROPHECIES AND PARABLES. The evangelists, in
reporting the events at Bethany and the solemn entrance of
Jesus into the city, had made it clear that the pilgrim and
teacher from Nazareth, a true man, subject to all the conditions and liabilities of the human predicament, was the messiah announced by the prophets of old, and the Son of God,
sent from his Father to save fallen men. For the time being,
the people appeared utterly divided, and Jesus expected it:
"I have not come to bring peace, but the sword" (Mtt 10:
34-36). The present hour was given to the powers of darkness, and the disciples had to be warned against despondency
and despair. The triumph would come only after the cross;
the "time of the Church" would not be exempt from ordeals,
and Christians had to raise their sights further and higher,

as they would follow their Master on the rugged paths of life. Thus the three days of passion week following the messianic entrance into Jerusalem would see the Master giving the last instructions to the disciples: prophecies, some of which would be accomplished within a few decades, or to the end of time, when Christ would return in power, and urgent appeals to vigilance and perseverance, on the familiar mode of parables.

The Synoptics have recorded in almost identical terms three instances of Jesus announcing his oncoming passion, death and resurrection: after the "confession" of Peter at Caesarea Philippi (Mtt 16:21-23; Mk 8:31-33; Lk 9:22), after the transfiguration (Mtt 17:22-23; Mk 9:30-32; Lk 9-44-45), and when Jesus and the twelve set out on their journey to Jerusalem (Mtt 20:17-19; Mk 10:32-34; Lk 18: 31-34). The mere prospect made Peter indignant. The words of Jesus met with total incomprehension on the part of the disciples. "They understood none of those things," writes St. Luke, "for these sayings were hidden from them." Not until after the resurrection would they understand, when two of them, dejectedly walking down the road to Emmaus, were joined by a mysterious traveller, who reproached them their incredulity: "O foolish men and slow of heart to believe all that the prophets have spoken!" And they heard the first catechesis from the very lips of Jesus himself, whom they recognized at the breaking of the bread (Luke 24:25-31).

Jesus' prophetic utterances, beyond the prediction of his now imminent passion, constitute the so-called "eschatological discourse" (Mtt 24:4-41; Mk 13:5-37; Lk 21:8-36). The occasion had been the admiring exclamations of the disciples at the sight of the temple, as they walked the steep path of the Mount of Olives on their way to or from Bethany (Mtt 24: 1-3; Mk 13:1-4; Lk 21:5-7), and Jesus' anguished call to Jerusalem: "Thou, killer of prophets . . . who stonest those who are sent to thee, how often would I have gathered thy children together, like a hen gathers her chickens under her wings, and thou wouldst not" (Mtt 23:37; Lk 13:34). But now Jerusalem was doomed, and of the magnificent structures of Herod there would not remain a stone left upon a stone.

A popular tradition purports to know the place where Jesus wept over the city, half-way up the crest of the Mount of Olives, directly above the Russian church of St. Mary Magdalene. From there the view extends, across the ravine of the Qidrôn, to the entire eastern front of the wall of Suleiman the Magnificent, and the gilded Dome of the Rock stands today where the House of Yahweh once stood, on the summit of Mount Môriah.

The discourse itself shows that there is a substantial agreement between Mark and Matthew, except for minor stylistic differences. Luke's version is somewhat freer, either because he used, in addition to the common tradition of Mark and Matthew, a source not known to them, or because, writing for the Greeks, he recorded Jesus' prophecies in terms which might be more readily understood by his readers. These prophecies form a chain, the first link of which had been Jesus' announcement of his passion, a few days hence; the second link is the ruin of Jerusalem and the destruction of the temple within a few decades; the third is the series of signs and portents of the end of this age and of the advent of Christ in glory. We have tried earlier to explain the economy of the prophetic revelation by tracing this literary pattern up to the late eschatology of the Old Testament and to the apocalyptic literature (see above, ch. 5).[10]

The discourses of Jesus as recorded in the Fourth Gospel are characterized by the rhythm of their periods. The style of the eschatological discourse is akin to that of the post-exilic prophets, Isaiah's second part, Jeremiah and Ezekiel's apocalyptic oracles. This contributes not a little towards unifying the short-range predictions of the discourse and the long-range prophecies announcing the end of the world. The former, under their stylistic garment, refer to events well within the grasp of the historian. The "false Christs", against whom Jesus warns his disciples, and which are mentioned in the epistles,[11] correspond to Jeremiah's false prophets, whom

[10] G. Barrois, *The Face of Christ in the Old Testament* (St. Vladimir's Seminary Press, 1974), pp. 131-132.

[11] False doctors and heretics, who will seduce the early Christians (2 Tim 4:3-4 and 2 Peter 2:1), and the "tools of the Antichrist" who will be the

Yahweh did not send, whose message is nothing but lies, hollow divination, and "the dreams of their heart", who lead the people astray or involve them in superstitious practises, like Ezekiel's prophetesses (Jer 14:14; 23:9-14; Ez 13:17-18).

The crisis was at hand. The revolt against the Romans, their procurators and their puppets, could explode at any moment, and to stay in Jerusalem would be madness! Christians would be suspect to all parties, dragged before sanhedrins and synagogue leaders, pagan authorities and petty officials, tempted to yield in utter despair; families would be divided, the children would denounce their parents. But "he who will endure to the end will be saved" (Mtt 24:13). Soon Jerusalem would be besieged by the legions of Vespasian, and the population torn asunder by rival factions. Daniel's "abomination of the desolation" (Dan 12:11) would be seen "in the holy place" (Mtt 24:15), "where it should not be" (Mk 13:14). Whether this "desolating sacrilege" (RSV) is a personal being or some pagan object of worship, we do not know, save that the allusion may have been intelligible to contemporaries: "Let the readers understand," wrote the evangelists.[12] Then the only safety would be in the flight to the mountains, by which is meant the maquis of Transjordan, from Moab to the Gôlan heights.[13] "Let those in Judaea flee and not tarry; they should not turn back to retrieve some valuable left behind," and please God that "it be not in winter, or on a sabbath!"

The perspective of the second part of the discourse ranges beyond history: there will be signs in the sun, it will be darkened; in the moon, it will lose its brilliance; in the stars, they will fall from heaven; there will be earthquakes and tidal

cause of a general apostasy in the last days, "are already in this world" (John 4:3; cf. 2 Thess 2:3-8).

[12] "The abomination of the desolation", either an evil character like the "wicked priest" of the Dead Sea Scrolls (probably Alexander Jannaeus), or a statue of *Jupiter Capitolinus*, when Jerusalem was renamed *Colonia Aelia Capitolina* after the second revolt of the Jews, A.D. 135. The event predicted by the Synoptics must fall in the interval between these two hypotheses, the former too early, the second too late.

[13] According to Eusebius (*Hist. eccl.* 3:5), Christians from the Jerusalem community had emigrated to the Hellenistic city of Pella, *Khirbet Fahîl*, opposite Scythopolis (Beisân).

waves, such as none has ever been recorded. The cosmic am-
plitude of the cataclysm defies all imagination. It will be
sudden, "like the lightning, which strikes from the east to the
west of the sky" (Mtt 24:27).

The anxious question of the apostles, "when will that
be?" is somehow irrelevant, for there will not be a "when"
any more. "Of the day and hour no one knows, not even the
angels in heaven, nor the Son, but the Father only" (Mtt
24:36; Mk 13:32; cf Acts 1:7). Then the conclusion of the
discourse cannot be anything else but a call to perseverance
and watchfulness, in faith, until the Son appears in glory, and
sends his angels "to gather the elect from the four winds, from
one end of heaven to the other" (Mtt 24:30-31; Mk 13:27).

The answer of Jesus to the question asked by the disciples
is at the origin of the theological problem of the double
knowledge of Christ; it involves the Christian dogma of the
incarnation: the personal Logos of God subsisting in a human
nature having its properties and its limitations, and in the
divine nature. Not to know the future is the lot of the humanity which Christ shares with us. St. Cyril of Alexandria wrote:
"When Christ said that he did not know the day and the hour
[of the parousia], he was speaking according to economy,
οἰκονομικῶς, preserving the due order of his humanity." [14]
This "ignorance" cannot be ascribed to the person of the
Logos, and is totally foreign to the absolute perfection of his
divine nature. This is the faith we profess, and we had better
not try to translate the mystery in terms of modern psychology.

The eschatological discourse is completed by a series of
parables which constitute the supreme teaching of Jesus in
the last days of his earthly life. The order in which they are
recorded by the Synoptics varies considerably; this, however,
is immaterial. They are familiar pieces, which could be easily
understood by the apostles and disciples, who had listened to
the parabolic teaching of the Master on the roads of Galilee.
One of the parables, about a fig tree, forms an integral part
of the eschatological discourse, and serves as a transition from
the prophetic teaching to the moral instruction of the listen-

[14] *Thesaurus de Sancta et Consubstantiali Trinitate* (written before A.D.
428). P.G. 75, col. 368.

ers. "From the fig tree learn its lesson, as soon as the branch becomes tender and brings forth leaves, you know that summer is near; so also, when you see all these [frightening] signs, you know that he [Christ] is near, at the very gates" (Mtt 24:32-33; Mk 13:28-29; Lk 21:29-31). Again the signs are given, not that Christians may draw a time-table of the future, but as a pressing exhortation to vigilance, the main theme of the parabolic instruction of the days preceeding the passion.

Another parable about a fig tree was prompted by an incident which St. Mark dates to Great and Holy Monday (Mtt 21:18-22, Mk 11:12-14, and 20-21). Coming from Bethany in the early morning, Jesus was hungry and saw a fig tree which already had leaves but no fruit — Mark notes naively that it was not the season. A curse on the tree! and on the spot it dried up. This is probably to be interpreted as one of the symbolic gestures of the Old Testament prophets, a prediction of Israel's rejection as being sterile and yielding no good works. The lesson is that the disciples must bear fruit; rather unexpectedly, Mark and Matthew link to that teaching a statement on the power of faith, which can make miracles. Now the story of the fig tree needed no commentary, and the long dissertations of some exegetes on fig varieties: early figs, summer figs, and the figs left on the tree in winter, are not illuminating; the evangelists did not write a treatise on pomology, and an element of fantasy belongs, anyway, in parabolic instruction.

Nor does the parable of the ten virgins (Mtt 25:1-13, modified by Luke 12:35-40) call for an anthropologist's exposition of nuptial rites among the Hebrews. The girls were supposed to meet the bridegroom and escort him to the house of the bride. Five of them failed through thoughtlessness and want of foresight. The lesson is clear: Christians are waiting for the second advent; let them be ready, "for the Son of man will be coming at an hour you do not expect." The parable has inspired our liturgists, and the first three days in Great and Holy Week are known in Orthodoxy as the "days of the bridegroom".[15] The story of the evil superintendent, who revels with his cronies while the estate-owner is away, teaches a grim lesson to those who have given up waiting through the long vigil of the Church " 'til he come" (Mtt 24:48-51; Lk 12:45-46). The parable of the vineyard workers who, in the prolonged absence of their master, beat his servants, kill his messengers, and murder his own son, is a prophecy of the rejection of the Jews as a nation, from whom the kingdom will be taken and given to those who will make it bear fruit (Mtt 21:33-43; Mk 12:1-11; Lk 20:9-18). The story of the laborers hired at different hours of the day, whose commentary by St. John Chrysostom we hear in the Paschal night, belongs to the same series. Christ will welcome the latecomer, who will receive the same wages as those who have worked from the morning; "so the last will be first, and the first last" (Mtt 20:1-16).[16]

THE SUPPER AND THE LAST VIGIL. We have examined in the first section of this chapter the problem of dating the last supper of Jesus with the twelve. We shall now direct our attention on its significance in the economy of salvation. The teaching of Christ during the first three days of Great and Holy Week has been a prophetic discourse on the ruin of Jerusalem, an announcement of the Old Testament institution coming to an end, and a prediction of the return of the Son of man on the last day of the first creation. Now the time has come for the sacrifice and the triumph. The concern of Christ is with his own, during the unmeasurable interval of time between the resurrection and the second advent. This is the time of the Church, which shall live by faith on remembering the Master. Christians would be subject to persecution, hostility, or — perhaps worse! — indifference; threatened by the temptation of adopting the ways of "the world",

---

[15] G. Barrois, *Scripture Readings in Orthodox Worship* (St. Vladimir's Seminary Press, 1977), pp. 78-79.

[16] There is no reason why the parable of the laborers should be interpreted as an allegory, in which all the details could be identified with historical events or characters, the eleventh-hour laborers, for instance, representing the Christians supplanting the Jews in the kingdom of God. As a matter of fact, there is no trace of allegorism in the homily of St. John Chrysostom.

renouncing the faith, and falling prey to schisms and rivalries. Under the olive trees of Gethsemane, Jesus was going to
live, within a few hours, the age-long ordeal of the Church,
as the total eclipse of his divinity began. He would experience
in his human nature, to a degree not shared by other men,
even the saints, that the flesh is weak, though the spirit is
deceptively willing (Mtt 26:41; Mk 14:38). Our sources will
be the Synoptics and St. John who, in to his usual manner,
avoids duplicating what had been already written by the other
evangelists but rather supplements their narratives and records *in extenso* Jesus' exhortations to the twelve and his
prayers to the Father.

We are at Bethany, on the morning of Great and Holy
Thursday. The commission given to the disciples to prepare
for what would be their last passover is related by the Synoptics in terms very similar to the episode of the little donkey
of Bethphage, borrowed for the procession of Palms (Mtt
26:17-19; Mk 14:12-16; Lk 22:8-13): "Go to town to a
certain man", πρὸς τὸν δεῖνα, not named but presumably
known by Jesus; you will meet a water-carrier, who will lead
you to a house where you will make the arrangements for the
feast; Peter and John were in charge, according to St. Luke.
We are somehow puzzled by the episode; but whether the
evangelists wished to imply that Jesus acted out of a supernatural knowledge,[17] or whether they reported, perhaps too
succinctly, the essentials of his instruction to the disciples, is
rather immaterial.

The description of the last supper of Jesus with the twelve,
extant in the Synoptics only, is brief and matter-of-fact, obviously a piece of the earliest Church teaching, drawing upon
the apostolic catechesis and the revelation to St. Paul (Mtt
26.26-29; Mk 14:17-25; Lk 22:14-20; 1 Cor 11:23-29). The
aim of our study is not a detailed comparison of the supper
with the Mosaic ritual and with the Jewish *Haggadah*; nor

---

[17] It is not clear whether the Synoptics intend here to ascribe to Jesus a
prophetic instinct, of which the Old Testament offers many examples; for
instance the "signs" given by Samuel to Saul searching for the lost asses of his
father: "Thou shalt meet two men near Rachel's tomb ... three men near the
oak of Tabor ... one carrying three kids; another, three loaves of bread; and
another, a skin of wine" (1 Sam 10:2-3).

does the manner in which our eucharistic liturgies use the words of Christ fall within the scope of our book. But one thing must be understood: when Jesus sat with the twelve at table, it was not out of a nostalgic remembering the days of Moses and the miraculous liberation from the servitude in Egypt. "Of a desire I have desired to eat this passover with you before I suffer, for I shall not eat it until it is fulfilled in the kingdom of God" (Luke 22:15-16). The whole thrust is not against, but with, the course of time. Jesus' intention was not to commemorate a ritual of the past, which was but a foreshadowing of the reality to come. The rites of passover were figures which would not be fulfilled through a chain of successive symbols, but through actual events: the supper with the twelve, an anticipation of our eucharist; the Divine Liturgy, an extension of the sacrifice in time and space, as the sacred body and the precious blood are handed unto us under the veil of the holy gifts; and the consummation of the mystery, the eternal reign of Christ in a re-created universe.

Whereas the Synoptics report only the institution of the eucharist, the Fourth Gospel, which omits it, supplements the Synoptics by recording what Jesus did and said in the upper room (John 13:31 to 16:33 and ch. 17). The warm human love which permeated all his actions awakened an immediate resonance in the soul of St. John, the beloved disciple. The washing of the feet of the twelve by their Master, omitted by the Synoptics (John 13:1-17), and which is liturgically re-enacted in many churches throughout Christendom, is called in Latin *mandatum*, from the words quoted by John 13:34, "I gave you a new commandment, *mandatum novum*, that you love one another as I have loved you." [18] In some religious orders of the western Church, the words which Jesus spoke are chanted, on the ferial tone of the lessons, under the name *Sermo Domini*, in the afternoon of Holy Thursday. These words of the Savior are recorded by St. John in the manner characteristic of the discourses pronounced on various occa-

[18] Hence, by corruption of the word *mandatum*, Great and Holy Thursday is called in England "Maundy Thursday". The ceremony of the washing of the feet is observed in the basilica of the Holy Sepulcher both by the Greeks and the Latins.

sions; they were words of farewell and call to perseverance in the faith in him who is "the Way, the Truth, and the Life"; the promise of a Comforter, Παράκλητος, who would inspire and guide the Church during the absence of the Master; an appeal to unity; and the assurance of the return of Christ on the last day. The discourse concludes with the prayer of Jesus for those who will believe in him and walk in the spirit of his precepts.

According to the Synoptics, Jesus and the twelve, before leaving the upper room, chanted the psalms of the Great Hallel, traditional conclusion of the *sêder* meal (Ps 113-118). By the light of the passover moon, they walked down to the olive-grove of Gethsemane, where they had been several times before, resting and praying. The vigil under the trees, reported by the four evangelists (Mtt 26:36-46; Mk 14:32-42; Lk 22:39-46; John 18:1-2), is the first act of the passion. The Son of God "empties himself" voluntarily, not of his divine nature, left to be discovered by men, but of the prerogatives of his divinity. Having taken up, by his incarnation, "the form of a slave" (Phil 2:7-8), he will not appear under other features than those of Isaiah's suffering servant (Is 50:5-6 and ch. 53). Not without a bitter conflict within his human soul: three times he prays his Father to be spared "this cup; however not what I will, but what thou wilt." The comforting angel mentioned by St. Luke will make him overcome this human distress, for our own sake. Meanwhile the disciples sleep, whom he had implored to pray, "lest they would enter into temptation" (Luke 22:43-46). The economy of the two natures in Christ, and the tension between the two wills, the human will and the divine will, are forcefully expressed by Pope Leo in his letter to Flavian (A.D. 449), which was used for the preparation of the dogma of Chalcedon; excerpts from the sermons on the passion form the lessons of the second nocturn on Thursday and Friday of the Holy Week in the Latin breviaries: "The Lord, by the words of his prayer, declared the truth and fulness of his twofold nature, showing from whence he could be reluctant to suffer, and whence it came that he would be willing."

The circumstances of Jesus' arrest are more detailed in

Luke and the Fourth Gospel than in Mark and Matthew (Mtt
26:47-56; Mk 14:43-52; Lk 22:47-53; John 18:1-12). Jesus
was still speaking to the apostles when the "cohort", ἡ σπεῖ-
ρα,[19] writes John, namely the detachment of the Roman gar-
rison in charge of the police, and some servants, ὑπηρέται,[20]
sent by the chief priests, rushed into the garden; it must have
looked like a posse, complete with torches, lanterns, and an
assortment of weapons, more than an orderly force, in spite
of John's mention of the χιλίαρχος, the "captain" in the
English versions. Judas, who led them, had given them a sign:
"The one I shall kiss, he is the man; seize him!" Then Jesus
came forward and said: "Whom do you seek?" — "Jesus of
Nazareth." — "I am he." — They drew back and fell to the
ground. Again Jesus asked them: "Whom do you seek?" —
"Jesus of Nazareth." — "I told you that I am he; so, if you
seek me, let these men go." A nightmarish scene follows:
Peter, brandishing a cutlass, cuts the right ear of the servant
of the high priest, a certain Malchus. A few words of Jesus
put an end to his apostle's ill-advised act of fencing. The
disciples scatter. A young man, moved by curiosity, watches
the scene, "with nothing but a sheet around his body"; the
guards seize him but, leaving his sheet in their hands, he
escapes stark naked (Mk 14:51-52). Was he not the evangelist himself, named John Mark in the Book of Acts? The
Christian community of Jerusalem used to meet in the town-
house of his mother after the resurrection (Acts 12:12).
The family may have owned the domain of Gethsemane, and
the young man, who had come to pass the night in a nearby
pavilion, was aroused by the din. Jesus, in bonds, was taken
straight to the residence of the high priest.

"CHRIST OUR PASCHA, SACRIFICED FOR US"
(1 Cor 5:7). A preliminary observation may be appropriate
here. Outbursts of antisemitism, whether out of blind passion
or deliberately instigated, which are the shame of our twentieth

[19] In modern Greek, a "band", a "gang".
[20] "The officers of the Jews" (English versions). In Greek, ὑπηρέται τῶν
'Ιουδαίων. In Hellenistic Judaism, the ὑπηρέτης is an inferior employee
in charge of maintaining good order in the synagogue, like the "Swiss" in
some French churches.

century, make us rightly apprehensive of generalizations
which serve too often as vehicles for ethnic, religious or class
prejudices. Our contemporaries show themselves increasingly
sensitive to charges and countercharges of unfairness. Jewish
and Christian scholars are intent upon evaluating the Gospel
record from this particular viewpoint, and professional lawyers have become interested in reviewing critically the trial
and condemnation of Jesus Christ, as we know them from
the four Gospels.[21] We cannot delay any further giving a
modicum of attention to a problem which bears on the Gospel
record as a whole, but more particularly on the interpretation
of the episodes of passion week, when the conflict between
Jesus and his enemies reached a climax.

In the time of the definitive redaction of the Gospel, the
differentiation of two groups of indigenous Palestinians, the
Jews and the young community of the Christians, had become
a fact. A polarization had taken place, as we may infer from
the episodes of the Book of Acts and from the epistles of
St. Paul. Jews resented the defection of some of their own
to the new faith. Politically minded Sadducees were alarmed
at whatever might serve as a pretext for drastic measures by
the Romans. Christians remembered with bitterness the role
played by some leaders in the drama of the passion. Generalizations, such as: "the Jews", "the priests", "the Pharisees",
"the scribes", were unavoidable; on the part of the evangelists, they were mostly descriptive. Jesus himself had used
very strong language to castigate the hypocrisy and duplicity
of his enemies. On the other hand, and of utmost importance
for a balanced judgment, are such episodes as the night-time
conversation of Christ with Nicodemus (John ch. 3) ; the same
Nicodemus' advice to his fellow sanhedrites (John 7:50-52) ;
the courageous intervention of Joseph of Arimathaea to obtain
from Pilate the body of the Crucified one; Nicodemus and
Joseph preparing it for burial and laying it in Joseph's own
tomb (Mtt 27:57-60; Mk 15:43-46; Lk 23:50-53; John 19:38-

---

[21] D. R. Catchpole, *The Trial of Jesus; A Study in the Gospels and Jewish
Historiography from 1770 to the Present Day* (Leyden, 1971). Haïm Cohn,
The Trial and Death of Jesus (English translation of the Hebrew original,
1971).

42); a few weeks later, the dissent of Rabbi Gamaliel in full Sanhedrin, when the high priest and the members of the assembly inclined toward having the apostles secretly murdered (Acts 5:34-39).

The four Gospels, in several brief passages, refer to the decision of the Jewish leaders to do away with Christ. They feared that his claim to be the Messiah and the Son of God, at a time when Galilean zealots threatened to revolt against the Romans, might bring retaliation against the entire nation. In the eyes of the priests, it was not merely a theological matter, but a burning political issue (Mtt 26:3-5; Mk 14:1-2; John 11:47-53). And not only Jesus should be put to death, but also Lazarus, an embarrassing witness (John 12:10-11). Was it not better that "one man should die for the people"? In saying this, Caiaphas was unwittingly a prophet, but the nation was not to be spared.

It is in connection with these intrigues that we meet the disquieting figure of Judas, waiting for Jesus to manifest himself openly as the Messiah. But Jesus appeared an incompetent revolutionist, letting the occasions pass, as he did after the raising of Lazarus or the triumphal procession of palms. Judas, feeling gravely compromised, let himself be bought by the chief priests and agreed to deliver Jesus into their hands for thirty silver shekels; as we already know, he was not particular in matters of honesty (Mtt 26:14-16; Mk 14:10-11; Lk 22:3-6).

St. Matthew alone relates the suicide of Judas (27:3-10). Stricken by remorse, Judas threw his shekels "into the temple", for the priests had refused to take them back, and he went and hanged himself; the priests had scruple to put that "blood-money" into the sacred treasury, and used it for purchasing the "field of the potter" as a burial ground for strangers. "Therefore that field has been called the field of blood even to this day." [22] St. Matthew, always eager to show the corres-

---

[22] "The field of blood". We see no good reason why this interpretation of the Aramaic *Haqêldamâ* preserved by Luke (Acts 1:19) and transcribed Ἀκελδαμάχ, should be rejected. The "potter's field" is the piece of land where the prophet Jeremiah purchased an earthenware jug and broke it, as an effective prophecy of the repudiation of Israel (Jer 19:1-15). The burial ground of *Hagêldamâ* has continued uninterrupted over the centuries. In the Latin

pondance of Old Testament oracles with the Gospel events, quotes here a prophecy of Zechariah which he attributes erroneously to Jeremiah: "They took the thirty silver shekels, the price of him that was appraised by the Benê Israel, and gave them for the field of the potter, as the Lord directed me" (Mtt 27:9-10, quoting Zech 11:12-13). The Book of Acts (1:19) gives a noticeably different version of the end of Judas: he, not the priests, bought the field, and the episode of the suicide abounds in gory details.

The late medieval and early Renaissance times in the west abound in devotional treatises whose purpose was to follow the Master from the atrium of Caiaphas to Golgotha. Authentic Gospel data are mixed with fragments of local folklore which the guides to the holy places — the *locorum monstratores* — recited to visitors always eager to know more and little concerned with historical validity. The ideal of many moderns is rather a televised presentation of facts, abstraction being made of Christian faith. We have already made it plain that we approach the subject from an entirely different point of view, starting from the faith of the Church. The very title of this section is excerpted from the *anaphora* of our liturgy; "Remembering all these things which have come to pass for us: the Cross, the Tomb, the Resurrection on the third day, the Ascension into heaven, the Sitting at the right hand, and the second and glorious Advent. . . ." We hold that there is no other way to the heart of the mystery but through the Church. Nothing can substitute for the "Twelve Gospels" we read or hear on Great and Holy Thursday, or the chant of the *Improperia* and of the Passion Gospel at the Mass of the Presanctified in the Latin office of "Good Friday".[23]

The four evangelists relate how Jesus, after his arrest in

Middle Ages it was a charnel house for the pilgrims who died in the hospice of the Knights Hospitalers. Remains of the vaults are still visible on the southern scarp of the *Gê-Hinnom* (*Ou. er-Rabâbi*) close to the Greek monastery of St. Onuphrios.

[23] The *improperia* are verses from Isaiah describing the ingratitude of the nation toward God, and the outrages inflicted upon his servant. They are chanted on Good Friday in alternation with the *Trisagion*, prior to the worship of the Cross, *Adoratio Sanctae Crucis*, and the Mass of the Presanctified.

the garden of Gethsemáne, was taken to the residence of the high priest, or of the high priests, says John, namely Annas and Caiaphas his son-in-law, who was in charge. In the courtyard, waiting for dawn, Peter, betrayed by his Galilean accent, denied knowing "that man", as Jesus had predicted. The cock's crowing brought him to his senses,[24] and Peter wept bitter tears. Then follow, in rapid succession: a "pre-trial" questioning of Jesus by the Sanhedrin, Caiaphas presiding; Jesus led to Pilate, who, learning that Jesus was a Galilean, sent him to Herod the tetrarch, who was eager to see the miracleworker everybody talked about; back to Pilate's tribunal for the formal hearing. The death sentence was pronounced, and Jesus was taken to be crucified.

It is not our intention to join the procession of the Jerusalem pilgrims along the *Via Dolorosa* for the "stations of the cross", whose number and location have varied considerably in the course of time due to the variations of the local folklore.[25] We would rather apply ourselves to discerning, beneath the detail of the Gospel narratives, the mystery of the incarnate Logos.

The entire course of Jesus' life had given evidence of his divinity. Prophecies had foreshadowed it. Voices from heaven had borne witness to it. His miracles had convinced those of his contemporaries who were unprejudiced. Healing their sick, he had declared his power to forgive sins, a prerogative of God. In his discussions with the Jews, he had proclaimed that "he was He", and to the beggar born blind, asking who was the Son of man who had opened his eyes, that he might

[24] Peter's denial, announced by Jesus (Mtt 26:34; Mk 14:30; Lk 22:34; John 13:38), actually described (Mtt 26:69-75; Mk 14:66-72; Lk 22:56-62; John 18:15-18, 25-27). The residence of the high priests has been variously localized in the southern quarters of Jerusalem. A Byzantine church commemorated St. Peter's tears of repentance, and became known in medieval Jerusalem as the church of St. Peter "at the cock's-crow", *in Gallicantu*. The modern church of the Assumptionists, built in the 1930s, stands on the ruins of a previous votive church. On the other hand, the little church of *Deir Zeitounieh* and a chapel, both in the Armenian quarter, witness to an ancient localization of both the "house of Annas" and the "palace of Caiaphas". See Vincent and Abel, *Jérusalem Nouvelle* (Paris, 1922), pp. 482-514.

[25] On the history of the Western devotion of the "Stations of the Cross", the *Via Sanctae Crucis*, see Vincent and Abel, *Jérusalem Nouvelle* (Paris, 1922), pp. 626-637.

believe in Him, he had answered: "It is he who speaks to thee" (John 9:36-38).

But now, a double veil hid the divinity of Christ: the veil of flesh, and his will to appear as no one else but the Suffering Servant of the prophecy of Isaiah. Only when challenged by his accusers and his judges would he reveal his divinity. To the high priests who adjured him by the Living God to tell whether he was the Christ, the Son of God, he answered: "Thou hast said", σὺ εἶπας, and he added a last prophetic statement, so that the Sanhedrites might understand that he was not merely their traditional human Messiah, but the "Lord". "Hereafter you shall see the Son of man sitting on the right hand of power and coming on the clouds of heaven" (Mtt 26:63-66; Mk 14:61-64; Lk 22:66-71). A blasphemy! The only verdict could be: Death!

Pilate, a typical colonial administrator, was not interested in the theological speculations of the Jews, for whom he had no sympathy. But their denunciation of Jesus, that he claimed to be king, touched a dangerous subject. Pilate's first question was: "Art thou the King of the Jews?" The answer was equally blunt: "Thou sayest", σὺ λέγεις — a manner of saying yes (Mtt 27:11-14; Mk 15:2-5; Lk 23:2-4; John 18:33-37). Pilate was superstitious, like all the Romans, and his wife had alarmed him with the report of a bad dream she had about "that just man" (Mtt 27-19). Pilate felt relieved in hearing that the kingdom of Jesus was "not of this world" (John 18:36-38); he dutifully registered the claim of "the accused" to his supernatural identity; he even tried to help him out, but was defeated by Jesus' deliberate silence. Dysmas, the "good thief", understood also but, unlike Pilate, he believed, and his faith would save him (Lk 23:42-43).

No human shall ever grasp the drama of the crucifixion: the eternal Son of God has become for our sake "the man of sorrows" of the prophecy of Isaiah. *Ecce homo*! Behold the man! Scourged, spat upon by the valets of the high priest; mocked by the Roman soldiery: a crown of thorns, a reed for a scepter, a scarlet rag for his royal robes, "Hail, king of the Jews!" Dragged to the rock of Golgotha, nailed to the cross which he was made to carry through the streets of the

city, challenged by the onlookers: "Aha, thou who destroyest
the temple and buildest it up in three days, come down from
the cross!" Abandoned by his friends, abandoned by his Father:
"My God, my God, why hast thou forsaken me?" *Eli, Eli,
lemâ sabachthani!* (Mtt 27:46; Mk 15:34), the very cry of
the anonymous martyr of Psalm 22. Some of the bystanders
had misunderstood Jesus' words and thought he was calling
Elias, for Elias (Elijah) was deemed to be the forerunner of
the Messiah to appear in the latter days. "When the sixth
hour had come", "from the sixth hour to the ninth hour",
there was darkness all over the land. A scene of apocalypse:
"The curtain of the temple was rent from top to bottom, the
earth shook, the rocks were split, the tombs were open; the
bodies of the saints who had fallen asleep were raised and
appeared to many" (Mtt 27'51-53; Mk 15-33; Lk 23:44-45).
The evangelists have attached a capital importance to these
cosmic phenomena. They mark the end of Old Testament
Judaism, which condemned itself while condemning Jesus
and causing him to be crucified. From then on, the economy
of the Mosaic covenant is superseded; no longer will a high
priest chosen from among men enter once a year into the Holy
of Holies and make atonement for his sins and the sins of
the people, but Christ, priest according to the order of Melchi-
sedech, enters with his own blood, once and for all, and in
this we have "a sure and steadfast anchor of the soul, a hope
that reaches into that which is within the veil" (Hebr 6:19).

The Fourth Gospel is alone to mention the presence of
St. John and the Theotokos at the foot of the cross, and the
supreme testament of Jesus entrusting his mother to the disciple (John 19:26-27). Jesus' last words are recorded by
the evangelists: "I thirst," "Father, into thy hands I com-
mend my spirit," "It is finished" (Lk 23:46; John 19:28-30).
"And Jesus bowed his head and gave up the ghost." The thrust
of Longinus' spear [26] into the side of the dead Christ closed
the Gospel of the passion according to St. John, fulfilling an

---

[26] The names of Longinus, and of Dysmas "the good thief", do not appear
in the canonical Gospels. The *crurifragium*, i.e. breaking the legs of those
crucified, was spared to Jesus, who had already expired. St. John sets this
detail in relation to a text of Exodus on the paschal lamb (Ex 12:46).

oracle of Zechariah, "They shall look to him whom they have
pierced" (John 19:34-37; Zech 12:10). "Truly", concluded
the centurion and his men, "this was the Son of God" (Mtt
27:54; Mk 15:39).

What follows contrasts with the hectic recording of the
passion events. We hear an even account of the burial, bared
to the essential facts (Mtt 27:57-66; Mk 15:42-47; Lk 23:
50-56; John 19:38-42). Joseph and Nicodemus obtained from
Pilate the permission to proceed with the burial without delay;
time was pressing: the high sabbath would begin at sunset;
they wrapped the body in a linen shroud with aromatic spices
which Nicodemus had brought, and laid it in the tomb which
Joseph had caused to be dug for himself in his garden, a few
steps from the rock of Golgotha; they rolled a huge stone at
the entrance of the funeral chamber, attentively watched by
the women, who planned to return after the sabbath with more
spices to complete the embalming. Now the sepulcher was
sealed; guards were posted at the request of the high priests
"until the third day", a futile guarantee against that resurrection which Jesus had announced: the "sign of Jonas", the
only one which would be given to "that adulterous generation" (Mtt 16:4; Lk 11:29).

No human being witnessed the resurrection. The myrrh-
bearing women and the apostles found the tomb empty. They
remembered that Jesus had told them how, on the third day,
he would rise from the dead. They heard angels saying: "He
is not here, he is risen." They believed, and they saw the
Master. Here is a fact, and a faith: not the end of a dream,
but the dawn of a new age, for "Christ is risen! Truly he
is risen!"

The Passing of Figures

Our survey of the Hebrew sanctuaries and of those episodes of Jesus' life which took place in the temple has made
us aware of the progress of divine revelation from the first
day of creation to the Amen of the Apocalypse. This progress
is not the result of a casual flow of happenings without an
ordaining Logos. Nor did God abandon schemes which proved
unsuccessful or had become obsolete, as if he had to try something else. "I am the Lord, I change not" (Malachi 3:6) and
"there is in Him neither change nor shadow of variableness"
(James 1:17). Whatever change there appears to be is but
the effect of a divine condescension to meet the requirements
of a growing mankind. "God, who allowed all the nations to
walk in their own ways", has never left them without guidance
(Acts 14:16-17). The economy of Providence consists in successive transpositions of the one theme: our salvation from
sin and death, and the pageant of biblical history makes us
assist to a continuous passing of figures such as each one of
them is pregnant with a reality hitherto veiled, whose actuali-
zation foreshadows a further revelation and a further achievement.

The first decisive event occurred in the fields of Ur of the
Chaldees and along the belt of cultivable lands bordering the
arid Syro-Arabian steppe. This was the road of the Aramaean
migration which brought Abraham and his family to the
"promised land", in the light of a revelation from the One
God, who would set them apart from all other peoples, from
the moon-worshippers, and be their savior.

The second crucial moment in the history of the Hebrews
is when their clans, gathered at Horeb, were constituted into
a single nation, and when Yahweh, the God who spoke to

Moses from the midst of the Burning Bush, revealed himself as the God whom Abraham had worshipped. From then on, Hebrew monotheism would find its grammar of expression in the Mosaic institution and the Sinaitic covenant.

With the crossing of the Jordan by the forces of Joshua, under the protection of the God who sits between the cherubim of the ark, the land of promise became the land of Israel in perpetual possession, conditional upon the faithfulness of the people.

The conquest of Jerusalem over the Jebusites endowed Yahweh with a permanent residence on the summit of Mount Môriah, where the faith of Abraham had been put to test. Yahweh would no longer depend on the hospitality of a tribe gaining custody over the ark over its rivals. Now the house of David, whose cradle had been Bethleem-Ephrata, would be custodian of the national sanctuary. Long after the destruction of the Solomonic temple, a savior, son of David, would rise and inaugurate the kingdom "which is not of this earth".

The collapse of the Judean monarchy brought about a necessary re-evaluation of saving values. The religion of Yahweh could no longer subsist on the robust realism of the past. The ark was no more. The worship at the temple was in danger of degenerating into a lifeless ritual and a sterile formalism. The post-exilic prophets looked increasingly beyond the narrow limits of the homeland toward the diaspora and the regions of the Gentiles. In order to live, Judaism had to spiritualize and universalize itself.

Then Christ was born, a descendant of David. He preached the good news of his Gospel in fulfillment of the Old Testament prophecies, on the roads of Palestine, in the synagogues and in the courts of the temple, on the days of the great Jewish festivals. But the sons and daughters of Zion would not be gathered under his protection in the shadow of the temple walls, of which he predicted that days were coming when not one stone would be left standing upon another. And Christ convened his own unto the "temple not made by hands", on the day of the final resurrection: all the elect, those from the twelve tribes of Israel, and "the great multitude which no man could number, standing before the throne" (Apoc

7:9). Since that Friday when the veil of the sanctuary was rent asunder, the darkness which enveloped the mysterious Presence in the Holy of Holies had been irremediably violated and, according to a local tradition quoted by Josephus, a voice was heard saying: "Let us depart from here!"

The resurrection of Christ marks a radical break between the economy of salvation in the Old Testament and in the New. The Synagogue counts its years from the creation of the world. We count our years from the birth of Christ. It is not only a question of eras; the very nature of time has changed. We have entered the initial phase of a new aeon and we look ahead for its consummation. Our time-reckoning is more like a count-down, even though we cannot predict the day and the hour which, as a man, Jesus himself ignored.

Failing to recognize Jesus as the Messiah, modern Judaism faces three options: the Messiah is still to come and he will assure the triumph of Israel in this world. This neither affirms nor denies the general resurrection — an old problem which had divided the Pharisees and the Sadducees in the time of Jesus. Or the Messiah is, so-to-speak, "de-historicized". He becomes an ideal personage who will appear in an indefinite future, with little relation to the predicament of our time. The Messiah may even not be a human being at all, but the symbol of a hoped-for perfect world of which an idealized Israel will be the agent, and its Scriptures the seed. There remains the option of political Zionism: a modern, secularized state claiming to be built on the foundation of the past but making abstraction of the biblical faith, at least in theory; hence its problems in matters of legislation: sabbath laws, marriage and divorce laws which, even if they are not dictated by the rabbinate, follow its rulings; not without disagreement between orthodox rabbis and their more liberal colleagues. The so-called "law of return" has even confronted the government with an un-answerable question, which may sound ludicrous: who after all, is a Jew?

The Christian Church has never lost from sight the real personality of Jesus Christ: no ethereal figure, but in truth the Messiah, son of David according to the flesh. We may not set the "Jesus of history" in opposition to the "Jesus of faith", the One Lord, *Jesus the Christ*. His death and resurrection have changed the meaning of history. Christians will live between the times "till he come" to reign over a re-created universe, when the number of the elect will have been made perfect. "Even so come, Lord Jesus!"